EASTERN WISDOM

EASTERN WISDOM

AN ILLUSTRATED GUIDE TO THE RELIGIONS
AND PHILOSOPHIES OF THE EAST

C. SCOTT LITTLETON, GENERAL EDITOR

A Henry Holt Reference Book
HENRY HOLT AND COMPANY
NEW YORK

Henry Holt and Company, Inc.
Publishers since 1866
115 West 18th Street
New York, New York 10011

Henry Holt ® is a registered trademark of Henry Holt and Company, Inc.

Originally published in the United Kingdom in 1996 by Macmillan Publishers under the title *The Sacred East*.

Library of Congress Cataloging-in-Publication Data
Eastern wisdom: an illustrated guide to the religions and philosophies of the East/C. Scott Littleton, general editor.
p. cm.
Includes bibliographical references and index.
1. Asia—Religion. 2. Philosophy, Oriental.
1. Littleton, C. Scott.
BL1032.E38 1996   95-38082
291'.095—dc20   CIP

ISBN 0-8050-4647-X

Henry Holt books are available for special promotions and premiums. For details contact: Director, Special Markets.

First American Edition—1996

Conceived, edited, and designed by Duncan Baird Publishers, England

Editor: Daphne Bien Tebbe
Assistant editor: Lucy Rix
Designer: Sue Bush
Picture research:
Cecilia Weston-Baker
Map illustration and decorative borders: Lorrraine Harrison
Commissioned calligraphy:
Yukki Yaura

Typeset in Times NR MT and Rotis Sans Serif.
Colour reproduction by Bright Arts, Hong Kong.
Printed in Singapore by Imago Publishing Limited.

10 9 8 7 6 5 4 3 2 1

Contents

INTRODUCTION 6
Professor C. Scott Littleton

INTRODUCTION

Hinduism, Buddhism, Confucianism, Daoism and Shinto together command the devotion of well over half of the human race, and the range and variation within each of these religious and philosophical traditions is vast. In this book we have therefore chosen to emphasize key themes and ideas rather than to provide a plethora of details about specific beliefs and practices.

We have also have attempted to ground these five traditions in the cultural and historical milieux that produced them, and to comment, where relevant, on the impact they have had on the societies that have subsequently adopted them. Indeed, without at least some understanding of these five traditions, it is impossible to comprehend fully the course of civilization in India, China and Japan, as well as in a host of other east and Southeast Asian countries.

Yet above and beyond their immediate historical and cultural significance, the religious and philosophical beliefs we shall shortly explore – that is, those which comprise what may be called "Eastern wisdom" – have something important to say to all of us, no matter what portion of the globe we call home; and it is hoped that the reader will come away from this book with new insights into the myriad ways in which human beings have come to grips with what the eminent Protestant theologian Paul Tillich (1886–1965) called matters of "ultimate concern". For essentially, Hinduism, Buddhism, Confucianism, Daoism, and Shinto – like all religious and philosophical systems, Eastern or Western – attempt to provide answers to the fundamental questions that

This 18th-century Chinese painting shows Confucius (right) holding the baby Buddha, while the Daoist sage Lao Zi looks on. Each of these figures has had an immeasurable influence on the religious, philosophical and cultural life of east Asia.

have confronted human beings everywhere from time immemorial: Where do we come from? What is our purpose? What is virtue? Why do we suffer pain and death? And, perhaps most important of all, how can we achieve salvation?

We begin with Hinduism, which, directly or indirectly, has profoundly influenced the religious and philosophical traditions of almost every civilization in Asia. It is, in many respects, the primary font of "Eastern wisdom", and has been such since the late 18th century, when Sir William Jones (1746–1794), the father of modern historical linguistics, first attempted to make sense out of the Indian epic known as the *Mahabharata*. This recognition was furthered by 19th-century orientalists such as Friedrich Max Müller (1823–1900), a distinguished Sanskrit scholar and historian of religion who edited a monumental, fifty-volume series called *The Sacred Books of the East* (1876–1911).

The roots of the Hindu tradition lie deep in the soil of northern India. They reflect a synthesis of the beliefs and practices of the indigenous population of the Indian subcontinent and those that were introduced some 3500 years ago by the Indo-European-speaking Aryans, whose religious beliefs, as reflected in the Rig Veda (*c*.1200 BCE) and other ancient Indian texts, were not all that dissimilar to those of the ancient Greeks. Shortly after the beginning of the Common Era, Hinduism spread into Southeast Asia travelling as far east as the island of Bali in Indonesia. While few parts of that region (Bali being one of them) still practise the faith, its impact remains profound; indeed, it is no accident that the Thai and other Southeast Asian aesthetic traditions, which are expressed in dance, theatre and so on, are based on the other great Hindu epic, the *Ramayana*.

No human belief system is more complex or variegated than Hinduism; indeed, it has been said that there are perhaps as many "little" Hindu traditions as there are villages in India (around

The Hindu god Vishnu, the protector of the universe, was incarnated in a series of ten avatars, or divine forerunners. This 18th-century statue depicts the avatar Matsya, the fish, who protected humankind from a great flood that came about soon after creation.

3.2 million). Nevertheless, underlying this vast array of local cults and rituals is a "great tradition", which includes a tremendous body of sacred Sanskrit literature ranging from philosophical disquisitions (such as the *Bhagavad Gita*, or "Song of the Lord") to epic tales of lost kingdoms regained and lost brides recovered (such as the *Mahabharata* and the *Ramayana*). Contained in this literature are the fundamental theological tenets that have shaped Hindu thought for millennia: the transmigration of souls, the wheel of karma and the concept of nirvana – the ultimate release from the pain of death and rebirth.

Buddhism, the great "daughter religion" of Hinduism, was first preached in northern India in the late 6th and early 5th centuries BCE by Siddhartha Gautama, the "historical Buddha", or "Enlightened One". Early on, the Buddhist community split into two major factions, which have come to be known as the "Greater" and "Lesser Vehicles" that is – the Mahayana and Theravada (or Hinayana) traditions. The Theravada, which emphasizes meditation and monasticism, has become the primary religion of Southeast Asia, from Burma to Cambodia and, in pre-modern times, Indonesia as well; while the Mahayana, which emphasizes universal salvation and a host of quasi-divinities called *bodhisattvas*, spread north and east, first to China, and then to Korea and Japan. In the process of expansion, Buddhism has become a transcultural religion and has managed to coexist with indigenous beliefs and practices throughout the regions it has penetrated, especially in east Asia. At the same time, it has spread the fundamental ideas of Hinduism – profoundly modified, of course – in much the same way that Christianity has spread the fundamental ideas of its parent religion, Judaism, to almost every corner of the globe.

Two of the east Asian traditions with which Buddhism has coexisted, Confucianism and Daoism, are rooted in China.

A 15th–16th-century gilt figure of the Buddha. He is shown in the lotus position, a meditative posture associated with most forms of Buddhism.

Confucianism, which is not really a religion in the strict sense of the word, has itself also travelled widely and has profoundly influenced the way in which east Asians look at the world, and especially human relationships. It originated in the thought of the 6th-century BCE Chinese philosopher Kong Fu-zi, dubbed Confucius by Jesuit missionaries in the 16th century. In *The Analects* and other classic works, Confucius outlined a code of human conduct that continues to shape the way in which east Asians structure both their personal and political relationships. Indeed, the Master's emphasis on learning, and the veneration of those who dispense it, is still a cornerstone of east Asian culture, and in large measure accounts for the high value that the Chinese, Japanese and Koreans, as well as the Vietnamese, who also adopted Confucianism, have traditionally placed on education.

A Confucian analect: "To learn without thinking is fatal but to think without learning is just as bad." Such aphorisms form the basis of Confucian philosophy and underscore the importance that all Confucian societies have placed on education.

The second Chinese tradition, Daoism, is traditionally ascribed to the semi-legendary philosopher Lao Zi, who may have been an older contemporary of Confucius, but in fact it is probably much more ancient. Daoism is also far more mystical and esoteric than Confucianism; indeed, in some respects the *Dao*, which literally means "the Way", is as meditative and inward-looking a path as any to be found in Buddhism and Hinduism. Although it has not had the same impact on east Asia as Confucianism, Daoism's influence can be detected in both the Korean and Japanese traditions: as we shall see, several Daoist gods are included in the traditional Japanese pantheon.

This brings us to our final example of Eastern belief: Shinto, or the "Way of the Gods", which is the indigenous Japanese belief system. Deeply embedded in the Japanese consciousness, Shinto has managed to survive the impact of both Buddhism and Confucianism, as well as of Daoism, for the past 1500 years.

Despite the fact that it is not primarily concerned with the great mysteries of existence – that is, the afterlife, ultimate salvation, and so on – Shinto nevertheless still plays an extremely important part in shaping the spirituality of Japanese people, especially what might be called the spirituality of everyday life as opposed to a spirituality that focuses on salvation and the afterlife. The Japanese goal of achieving harmony (*wa*), while reflecting the imported ideas of Confucius, *et alia*, is in large measure predicated on the ancient Shinto ideal of achieving a balance within the realm of nature between humankind and the *kami* (gods) – a balance in which each element supports the other for the good of the whole.

Some might be tempted to argue that the notion of "Eastern wisdom" implied by this book, despite our attempt to move beyond the narrow confines of religion *per se* and accommodate the thoroughly secular wisdom promulgated by Confucius and his followers, smacks of what the writer and critic Edward W. Said (born 1935) has called "Orientalism": that is, the heavily romanticized – and, at the same time, condescending and intellectually imperialistic – attitude toward "the Orient" so commonly encountered among Westerners who have attempted to come to grips with non-Western religions and philosophies. Indeed, ever since Max Müller and other 19th-century scholars translated the principal "Eastern" religious texts, these belief systems have occupied an ambivalent position in the Western consciousness. On the one hand, they have typically been perceived as wholly "other" – that is, the antithesis of all that is logical and rational, especially when juxtaposed with the indigenous religious and philosophical traditions of the West (the Judeo-Christian tradition, Platonism, Aristotelian logic, and so on). On the other hand, "Eastern" religious traditions, such as Zen, have been widely embraced as prime sources of personal and spiritual enlightenment and have given new meaning to the ancient phrase *lux ex orienti*: "light from the East". In recent

Shou Lao, the Daoist god of longevity, holding a peach – a symbol of long life.

years, a variety of Asian philosophies and disciplines, such as Kundalini yoga, the Tibetan Buddhist notion of "guided imagery", the ancient Chinese divinatory technique expounded in the *Yi Jing* (*I Ching*) and the Nichiren Shoshu sect of Japanese Buddhism, have captured the Western imagination and continue to challenge the ways in which we conceive of reality.

However, as our knowledge of both Eastern traditions and the cultures that produced them has deepened and expanded, especially in the course of the last half-century or so, we are now in a position to assess them more objectively. Hinduism, Buddhism, Confucianism, Daoism and Shinto are profoundly different from Western spiritual and intellectual traditions. But as we mentioned at the outset, it is now possible to see these Asian traditions simply as alternative ways of approaching Tillich's "ultimate concern", and of coming to grips with the fundamental questions of origin, purpose, death and salvation. They are neither wholly "other" nor intrinsically more spiritual – or "light-giving" – than their Western counterparts.

In sum, it is hoped that the five manifestations of "Eastern wisdom" that are described in this book will offer the reader a more profound appreciation of both the unity and the diversity of human spirituality and the quest – Western as well as Eastern – for enlightenment, harmony, virtue and salvation.

C. Scott Littleton

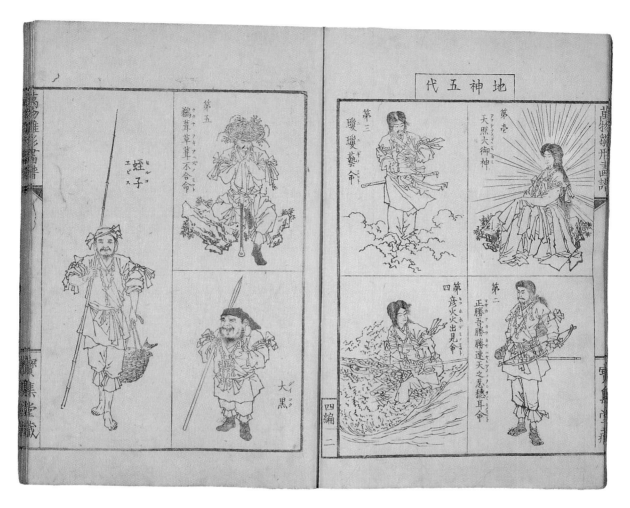

The Japanese imperial family is believed to be descended from the sun goddess, Amaterasu-omikami, head of the Shinto pantheon, and this 19th-century Japanese print traces her lineage to the legendary first emperor. The figures in the right-hand panel are Amaterasu (top right); her son, Masa-katsu-no-mikoto (bottom right); her grandson, Honiningi (top left); and Honiningi's son Ho-wori (bottom left). The figure in the upper right of the left-hand panel is Uka-ya-buki-ezu-no-mi-kami, father of the first Japanese emperor, Jimmu-tenno. The print also shows Ebisu (far left), one of the "Seven Lucky Gods" (Shichifukujin) of Shinto, who carries a fishing-rod and a sea bream, and is associated with prosperity and abundance. To his lower right is Daikoku, the "Great Lord of the Country", who, like Ebisu, is associated with material well-being.

HINDUISM

The Hindu religious tradition has a rich and complex history, with origins that extend as far back as the 3rd millennium BCE, when the Mohenjo-daro and Harappan civilizations were thriving in the fertile valleys of the Indus River (see map, p.17). Around 1500BCE, the nomadic Aryans entered the Indian subcontinent from Persia, introducing new beliefs, customs and social structures to the agriculturally-based Indus Valley communities. The interaction of the Aryans with the Indus Valley peoples, as well as with Dravidian culture (now dominant in southern India), began a process of spiritual development, which has led to the distinct strands that today are collectively referred to as Hinduism.

The word "Hindu" derives from *Sindhu*, the Persian name for the Indus River, and originally was used by outsiders to refer to the people who lived in that region. Only in recent centuries has it come to represent a more self-conscious identity for those who believe in *sanatana dharma*, the eternal and divine ordering of the cosmos as revealed in the Vedas, the sacred texts of the Hindus.

The archaeological evidence from the Indus Valley region has led scholars to speculate about the relation of these early cultures to modern Hinduism. In Mohenjo-daro the excavations of a bathing tank, as well as of advanced drainage systems, suggest that there was an emphasis on personal or ritual cleanliness, which is also significant to Hinduism. Terracotta female figures

In this 18th-century painting, women celebrate the spring festival of Holi by throwing coloured waters and powder. The festival, which takes place on the day of the full moon in March, is an occasion on which Hindu restrictions on caste, sex, age and status are lifted.

found in the Indus Valley indicate that there may have been a cult of goddess worship, possibly connected to the sustained reverence of the goddess in India today; and soapstone seals feature a male figure whom scholars refer to as proto-Shiva, because of his striking similarities to the later Hindu god Shiva.

The Aryan contribution to the development of Hinduism is illuminated primarily by the Vedas. The Aryans' language developed into classical Sanskrit, the principal language of orthodox Hinduism; and their tribal system evolved into the more formalized system of social classes. The Rig Veda suggests that this ordering of classes originated in the primeval sacrifice of the cosmic man (*purusha*). From his mouth came the highest-ranking, priestly class (*brahmins*). The warriors and rulers (*kshatriyas*) came from his two arms; the merchants and farmers (*vaishyas*) from his thighs; and the servant class (*shudras*) from his feet. This image has been used to demonstrate the organic nature of the system, according to which each class contributes in a specific way to the orderly functioning of society. In Hinduism, the class (*varna*) system is related to the present-day caste (*jati*) system, which is based on birth-groups and occupations, with the priest in the pre-eminent role. Rebellion against caste and against the elitism of Vedic sacrifice led to the beginnings of the Buddhist and Jain religions in India. It also provoked a reformulation of Hindu ideas, including a strong devotional movement, which was anti-caste and anti-ritual. Nevertheless, the concerns of hierarchy, specialized duties (*dharma*), ritual and priestly functions still feature prominently in the tradition.

Hinduism takes many different forms, embraces a variety of religious lifestyles and practices and turns to a range of authorities for guidance on spiritual and ethical matters. It has withstood many challenges and absorbed as well as transformed ideas from both within and outside its culture. Hindu kingdoms were once strong in much of Southeast Asia, and the Indonesian island of Bali is still largely Hindu. However, Hinduism has never really been a missionary religion, and today it remains very much tied to Indian culture and peoples, whether they live in Nepal, South Africa, the East Indies, Great Britain or the United States.

THE SACRED GEOGRAPHY OF HINDU INDIA

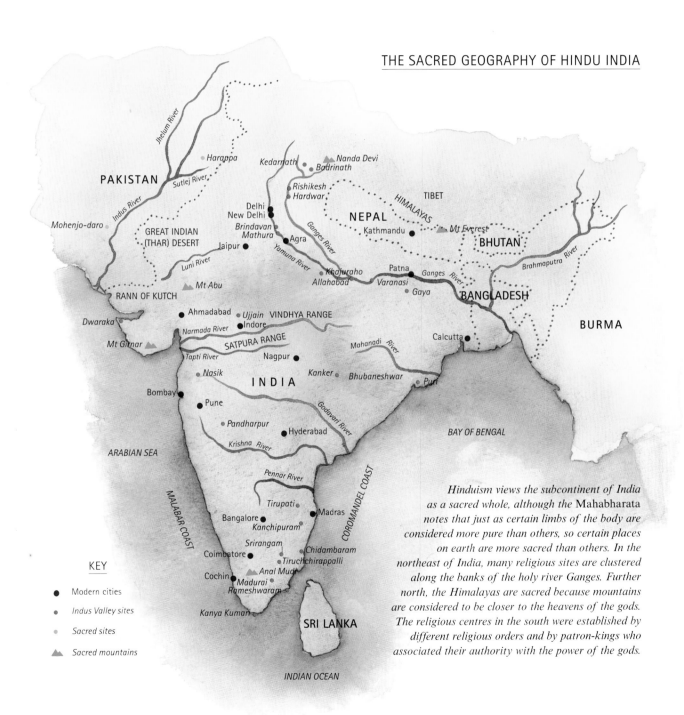

Hinduism views the subcontinent of India as a sacred whole, although the Mahabharata *notes that just as certain limbs of the body are considered more pure than others, so certain places on earth are more sacred than others. In the northeast of India, many religious sites are clustered along the banks of the holy river Ganges. Further north, the Himalayas are sacred because mountains are considered to be closer to the heavens of the gods. The religious centres in the south were established by different religious orders and by patron-kings who associated their authority with the power of the gods.*

KEY

●   Modern cities

•   *Indus Valley sites*

•   *Sacred sites*

▲   *Sacred mountains*

THE SELF AND THE ABSOLUTE

Hindu philosophical thought is characterized by a belief in the principle of *brahman*, the "universal soul". Uncreated, limitless, all-embracing and eternal, *brahman* is the ultimate reality: it is the subtle essence that underlies the universe; and, at the same time, it constitutes the innermost self or soul (*atman*) of each individual.

In the older Vedic religion, the term *brahman* referred to various forms of sacred power, which were manifested in Vedic ritual. Speculation on this sacred power led to contemplation of the connections that link the elements of ritual with both the macrocosm of external nature and the microcosm of the inner life of the individual. Such introspection culminated in the belief that there is a single essence (*brahman*) that underlies all existence and animates all living beings.

A person's realization of the identity and unity of *atman* and *brahman* is believed to bring about liberation (*moksha*; see p.30), because in that moment he or she is freed from all restraints of the mind and body, and thereby transcends all distinctions. Both the *Upanishads* (see p.20) and later systems of Hindu philosophy emphasize the central role of knowledge in the attainment of *moksha*, even while they differ from each other on the practical means that make such knowledge possible.

To realize that *brahman* and *atman* are ultimately the same is no easy task. The *Chandogya Upanishad* likens the learning process to crossing the ocean of suffering. An individual comes to know *brahman* through meditating on the nature of the self, but ultimately *brahman* is indefinable, because to define *brahman* would be to limit it. This view of *brahman* hints at a metaphorical paradox. If *brahman* is indeed infinite and limitless, encompassing the variety of the whole world, then it must be the source of

the universe, as the *Chandogya Upanishad* teaches. However, as the one true absolute, this same *brahman* is spoken of as remaining transcendent, beyond all differences. How, then, can such a single reality account for the diversity of the world? How can a single consciousness constitute the *atman* within different individuals without itself being divided? Later systems of philosophy wrestled with these questions.

The Vedanta school of philosophy specialized in the critical interpretation of the *Upanishads*, upholding the doctrine of *brahman* as the ground of all being. However, there were several schools within this system, and these differed from each other precisely on the questions of the relation between the one *brahman* and the diversity of creation and, in particular, of the relation between the universal *brahman* and the individual *atman*. Many early schools of formal Vedanta avoided straightforward answers. Individual souls are bound in misery, they maintained, because of the difference between *brahman* and *atman*; at the same time, however, this suffering

A page from a manuscript of the Sama Veda, with hymns that were sung during Vedic fire sacrifice. A later part of the Sama Veda, the Chandogya Upanishad, *examines Vedic ritual and the relationship between the inner spiritual world and the external worlds of nature and ritual.*

is due to people's ignorance (*avidya*) of the essential non-difference between *brahman* and *atman*.

The role of ignorance was stressed by later schools. In one major version of Vedanta, the 8th-century philosopher Shankara argued that the ordinary world as individuals perceive it is essentially an illusion, based on a fundamental error in knowledge. On the level of ultimate reality, only *brahman* exists, and this undivided consciousness is the true identity of each individual. Shankara's stance is called *advaita* (non-dualism), and is associated with the related doctrine that liberation arises from knowledge alone, not from action (*jnana-marga*; see p.30).

Other Vedanta schools have opposed Shankara, objecting to his insistence on the absence of all differences and maintaining that the distinction between god and god's devotees must be retained.

The Calcutta botanical gardens contain the oldest sacred banyan tree in India. In a passage from the Chandogya Upanishad, *a father tries to impart to his son the divine wisdom about the nature of the self by likening the fruit of the banyan tree to* atman *and the indiscernible substance within its seeds, responsible for its existence, to* brahman.

The most influential of these schools was led by the Vaishnava teacher Ramanuja (1017–1137), who took the stance of *vishishtadvaita* (qualified non-dualism). Ramanuja taught that the individual soul is not identical with god and, therefore, that a devotee may worship god even after liberation. In this tradition *moksha* is still viewed as being dependent upon a realization of the true nature of the self, but it is believed to be attainable through *bhakti* (devotion; see p.31), which involves the constant remembering of god or the surrender of the individual self to god.

SACRED TEXTS

A page from a 15th-century manuscript of the Rig Veda, the oldest (c.1200BCE) and best-known of the four Vedas.

The sacred texts of the Hindus examine almost every aspect of life, both human and divine. While numerous religious texts are popular among the different sectarian and regional traditions of Hinduism, there are some ancient and classical works that are considered to be especially authoritative. These texts are divided into two categories, *shruti* (hearing) and *smriti* (remembering), based on their traditional means of transmission.

The oldest and most revered of Hindu texts are the Vedas, in which the roots of Hindu wisdom and teaching are found. The actual use of these texts may be infrequent in the lives of many Hindus, but the concept of Veda (Knowledge) as a timeless body of revelation has served as the nucleus of some of the most distinctive features of Indian thought.

Composed by the Aryans, the Vedas were transmitted orally and are known as *shruti* (hearing). Not only the contents of these texts but also the sounds of the words themselves are considered sacred. They are believed to be of divine origin, containing eternal truths of the universe that were revealed to – heard by – *rishis* (seers) and sages, who preserved and passed on the sacred knowledge.

The Vedas are traditionally arranged into four collections. The Rig Veda contains more than 1000 hymns in praise of thirty-three gods and refers to rituals associated with these gods. Sacrifice was the main form of worship in Vedic times, and the Sama Veda sets the verses of the Rig Veda to music, to be sung during sacrificial rites. The Yajur Veda contains formulaic verses that were recited by the priest who oversaw the Vedic sacrifice. The fourth Veda, the Atharva, is a collection of charms and incantations.

Each of the four Vedas contains supplementary texts – *Brahmanas*, *Aranyakas* and *Upanishads* – which contributed to the development of Hindu beliefs. The *Brahmanas* are rich in narrative tales and technical discussions about sacrificial rites; the *Aranyakas* (forest treatises) contain more esoteric ritual formulas for the spiritually advanced, who favoured withdrawal from the world; and the *Upanishads* focus on questions of the self and the self's relationship with the cosmos. In these philosophical texts, the concept of *brahman* as a world-soul pervading the universe and each individual being (*atman*) is developed (see pp.18–19), while the need for ritualized sacrifice progressively diminishes.

A second category of authoritative sacred texts is collectively known as *smriti* (remembering) and, in contrast to the Vedas, these texts, although divinely inspired, were authored by humans. The *smriti* texts tend to be more accessible than the Vedas and, thus, many of them are popularly remembered and passed from generation to generation. They include the *Mahabharata* (see p.23), the *Ramayana* (see p.22) and the *Puranas*, which detail the cycles of creation and destruction of the world, provide genealogies of kings and gods, and usually highlight the activities of a particular deity. Various *sutras* and *dharma-shastras*, moral and legal guidebooks on proper conduct, also fall into this category.

The *smriti* tradition popularized the teachings of the Vedas, making the divine wisdom more relevant to the lives of ordinary human beings. The earlier Vedic texts revealed a religious tradition centred around sacrificial ritual as a means of addressing and appeasing the gods. The later Vedic texts, particularly the *Upanishads*, understood the divine as the omnipotent and impersonal *brahman*. However, in the *smriti* texts god is imagined to be much more personal, entering into the lives of humans by creating them, loving them, inspiring them to worship and ultimately, through divine grace, saving them. Verses from the *smriti* texts are often recited in an individual's daily meditation, and the stories from these texts are repeated by priests, grandmothers and storytellers as a means of inspiring moral living.

THE MYSTIC SYLLABLE *OM*

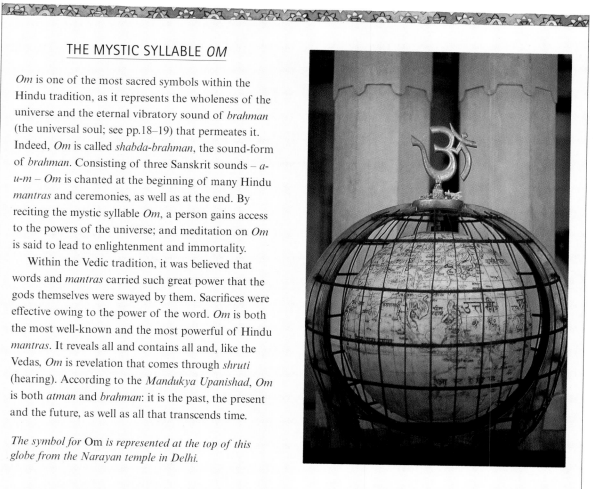

Om is one of the most sacred symbols within the Hindu tradition, as it represents the wholeness of the universe and the eternal vibratory sound of *brahman* (the universal soul; see pp.18–19) that permeates it. Indeed, *Om* is called *shabda-brahman*, the sound-form of *brahman*. Consisting of three Sanskrit sounds – *a-u-m* – *Om* is chanted at the beginning of many Hindu *mantras* and ceremonies, as well as at the end. By reciting the mystic syllable *Om*, a person gains access to the powers of the universe; and meditation on *Om* is said to lead to enlightenment and immortality.

Within the Vedic tradition, it was believed that words and *mantras* carried such great power that the gods themselves were swayed by them. Sacrifices were effective owing to the power of the word. *Om* is both the most well-known and the most powerful of Hindu *mantras*. It reveals all and contains all and, like the Vedas, *Om* is revelation that comes through *shruti* (hearing). According to the *Mandukya Upanishad*, *Om* is both *atman* and *brahman*: it is the past, the present and the future, as well as all that transcends time.

The symbol for Om *is represented at the top of this globe from the Narayan temple in Delhi.*

THE *RAMAYANA*

By far the best known and best loved of Hindu legends, the *Ramayana* has its origins in a heroic ballad about a great prince from the kingdom of Ayodhya. This epic narrative of the triumph of good over evil is traditionally attributed to the sage Valmiki, but it has taken many forms and its story has been told and retold in many different vernaculars and media, from dance-dramas and puppet shows to television serials. Both entertaining and didactic, the *Ramayana* has become the focus of spiritual devotions for those Vaishnavas (devotees of Vishnu) who worship Rama (see p.37) as an avatar of Vishnu (see p.34). It is believed that Vishnu was incarnated as Rama in order to destroy the forces of evil that were represented by the demon Ravana, and to restore a harmony that had been disrupted.

The story begins with the birth of Rama, son of King Dasharatha of Ayodhya. Dasharatha has three wives, and Rama is his eldest son, born of his wife Kausalya. Rama's stepbrothers include Bharata and Lakshmana. After his marriage to the beautiful Sita, daughter of King Janaka, Rama prepares to succeed his father on the throne. However, Bharata's mother, eager to see her own son on the throne, reminds King Dasharatha that he owes her two wishes, and insists that he fulfil them immediately. Her wishes are that Rama be exiled to the forest for fourteen years and that her son, Bharata, ascend the throne. The king is

The Rama-Lila, *a dance-drama that presents episodes from the* Ramayana, *is popularly performed throughout India and parts of south Asia. Here, a troop from Thailand performs the* Rama-Lila *in Bangkok.*

distraught over this request but is bound to keep his promise: he acquiesces, and later dies of grief. The perfect, obedient son, Rama honours the oath made by his father and agrees to be banished from the kingdom, relinquishing his claim to the throne. He is accompanied into the forest by Lakshmana, while Bharata, refusing to ascend the throne that is rightfully Rama's, acts as caretaker of the kingdom until Rama returns. Lakshmana and Bharata represent the ideal of family loyalty. Sita, who insists on accompanying Rama into exile, exhibits the behaviour of the model wife, devoting herself to her husband, in even the most adverse circumstances.

During his fourteen years in exile, Rama undergoes many trials and ordeals which test and enhance his virtues and skills. His greatest challenge concerns the abduction of his beloved wife, Sita, who is kidnapped by the demon Ravana and held captive on the island of Lanka. Rama enlists the aid of a band of monkeys, and Hanuman (see p.37), the monkey general, eventually finds Sita. In a bloody battle in which the many heads of Ravana are severed, Rama, Lakshmana and the monkeys defeat the army of demons. When Rama questions the purity and fidelity of his wife, who has been in the captivity of another man for several years, Sita proves her innocence and devotion by undergoing a fire ordeal. Rama and Sita return triumphant to Ayodhya, where Rama is crowned king.

THE *MAHABHARATA* AND THE *BHAGAVAD GITA*

A page from a 19th-century manuscript of the Bhagavad Gita, *showing Krishna, as charioteer, turning his head to speak to Arjuna. Both Hindus and non-Hindus have turned to the* Gita *for spiritual guidance, valuing its message that the cultivation of non-attachment leads to inner peace.*

The longest and most complex of India's epics, the *Mahabharata* (Great Epic of the Bharata Dynasty) offers an extensive study of the role of duty in human life. Parables, poetry and didactic essays cover topics related to history, statecraft, civil law, ethics, religious law, ritual and cosmology, all interwoven in a narrative about the turbulent war between two related dynasties. The text's 100,000 stanzas are filled with tales of the interaction of the human and the divine, in which ordinary lives are punctuated by both the miraculous and the demonic.

The basic plot concerns a conflict between the Pandavas and the Kauravas, the sons of two royal brothers. Each side lays claim to the throne, and a great battle for the kingdom ensues. The dreadful results of the actions taken by the *Mahabharata*'s heroes have led scholars to suggest that the moral of the poem lies in the notion of the ultimate futility of worldly life, as contrasted with the eternal reality of god. The message that liberation comes from god is central to the best-known and most influential passage in the *Mahabharata*, the *Bhagavad Gita*.

The *Bhagavad Gita* (Song of the Lord) captures a moment on the eve of the great *Mahabharata* war,

when Krishna reveals himself to be the supreme god. In this moment, one of the greatest and most popular Hindu treatises on the nature of the self and the universe unfolds in the form of a dialogue. About to enter battle against the Kauravas, Arjuna, one of the Pandava brothers, faces a moral and emotional crisis. Krishna, while admiring his concerns, explains that Arjuna's sorrow stems from ignorance about the self and the world: the true self is not the body, which is born, ages and dies, but rather is *atman* (the individual soul; see pp.18–19), which clothes itself in other bodies and lives eternally. Krishna emphasizes the importance of doing one's duty in order to maintain the order of the universe, and further advises Arjuna not to be attached to the consequences of his actions, but to have faith in god and the divine order.

The *Gita* preaches selfless action and devotion to god as paths to spiritual freedom, but the text itself is philosophically more complex. As a devotional meditation, many Hindus recite from the *Gita* daily; as an ethical text, it is consulted for its advice on proper conduct; and as a theological and philosophical text, it has been studied, interpreted and commented on by scholars from at least the 8th century.

CYCLES OF TIME AND CREATION

The Hindu tradition perceives the existence of the cosmos as one cycle within a framework of cycles: it may have been created and reach an end, but it represents only one turn in the perpetual "wheel of time", which revolves infinitely through successive cycles of creation and destruction. This doctrine of the cycles of time is a larger version of the notion of *samsara* (see p.26), the cycle of rebirth in which individual souls are repeatedly reincarnated.

The Hindu texts are full of varied and imaginative speculation about the primal cause and agent of the process of creation. One creation myth tells how the world came into being through the dismemberment of the "cosmic man"; another derives creation from a cosmic egg; a third attributes it to a dream of Brahma, the creator god; and a fourth tells how creation sprang from the tears of the demiurge Prajapati. The *Puranas* contain many stories that attribute creation to one of the supreme deities, particularly Shiva (see p.39), Vishnu (see p.34) and the Goddess (see pp.42–3); and the *Upanishads* include the philosophical speculations of the sages who struggled with this question of origins. Ultimately, these interpretations suggest that the source of creation is profoundly unknowable.

The details of creation are often vivid. In the myth in which the world issues from a cosmic egg, the upper half of the egg becomes the heavens, home of the gods, and the lower half becomes the mundane world of humans. In this world, humans live within a

ASTROLOGY

The ideas of the cycles of time and rebirth feature in many aspects of Hindu thought, including the practical details of astrology. Astrologers are consulted to predict the future, to explain the past and to determine the appropriate time for such events as marriage, breaking ground for a temple, undertaking a journey and moving into a new home.

The Hindu system recognizes the twelve signs of the zodiac, twenty-seven lunar mansions and nine "planets", each of which represents different characteristics.

A person's nativity under a specific planet, combined with other celestial phenomena, provides the information used to predict character, temperament and longevity, and to select a ritual name for a newborn child. Later, this chart is compared with that of potential partners to determine the prospects for a compatible and fruitful marriage.

In Hindu astrology the Moon (far left) represents emotion, Mars (centre) physical and mental capacity, and Mercury (right) communication and intellect. These planetary images come from the 16th-century Lagnacandrika.

series of concentric islands and seas, with Mount Meru, the axis of the universe, at the centre. The seven layers of heaven that hover above Mount Meru are occupied by seven different types of divine and semi-divine beings; and below the earth there are seven levels of netherworlds. The world rests on the head of a great serpent who is curled up on the back of the tortoise Kurma, who stands with each of his four feet on the back of a different elephant. The elephants in turn balance on the remains of a delicate eggshell. This vision depicts both the complexity and fragility of the world, and the importance of interdependence in sustaining it.

In a myth about the cyclic nature of creation, Vishnu, the protector of the universe, reclines on the back of a serpent in the middle of the ocean of dissolution and potentiality, napping in the period between the destruction of the world and its re-creation. When creation is about to begin again, a lotus emerges from Vishnu's navel. The creator god, Brahma, is enthroned upon this lotus.

This myth begins by reviewing the process of deterioration, represented by the four *yugas* (ages) during which the *dharma* (order) of the world declines. In the Krita Yuga, the Golden Age, there is no disease or hatred, humans live for 300 years, and *dharma* rests firmly on four legs. Following this, however, the universe goes through a process of degradation, concluding with the present age, the Kali Yuga, in which malice, deception and poverty reign and the world is devastated by floods and famines. *Dharma* wobbles unsteadily on one foot during the Kali Yuga, and life is so corrupt that people pray for the destroyer to bring an end to this miserable time. This cycle of four *yugas* covers 4,320,000 human years, and is called a *Mahayuga*. However, one *Mahayuga* is only the first stage in ever-increasing cycles upon cycles. Two-thousand *Mahayugas* is a single day and night in the life of Brahma; and this in turn corresponds to the cycles of creation and dissolution of the universe.

The cataclysm that comes at the end of Kali Yuga is described in various ways, but it is usually said to culminate in an all-consuming fire and incessant rains that cool the flames and turn the universe into an endless expanse of water. Vishnu then ends the winds and the rains and goes to sleep on the ocean of potentiality, which contains the future of creation. A night of Brahma (1000 *Mahayugas*) must pass before Vishnu awakes, and, through the agency of Brahma, the cycle of creation will begin again, overseen by Vishnu, the preserver.

In one popular Hindu myth, depicted in this 18th-century painting, creation resulted from the churning of the milk ocean. The serpent Vasuki was wrapped around the churning pole, which was then twisted by the gods and the demons. The god Vishnu took the form of Kurma, a tortoise, and supported the churning pole.

DHARMA AND KARMA

Hindu life is guided by a moral code that is exemplified by Hindu saints and heroes. It is believed that such key virtues as truthfulness, non-violence, purity, generosity and compassion should direct all activity, from the pursuit of *moksha* (spiritual liberation; see pp.30–31) to the pursuit of more mundane goals such as wealth, pleasure and happiness. The concepts of *dharma* and karma are at the centre of this system of ethics. Although Hinduism is not based on a single or definitive set of teachings, these two key ideas are generally accepted by members of the diverse religious schools within the tradition.

Dharma refers to the divine, social and ethical order of the universe, which is upheld or threatened by the actions of humans, gods and demons. Each individual has particular duties, related to status and class (see p.16), which he or she is responsible for fulfilling. By doing so, the individual helps to sustain the moral law and contributes to the maintenance of cosmic order (*dharma*).

Individual action (karma) plays a key role in the preservation of universal harmony, but it also significantly affects a person's involvement in the social and material world. According to the law of karma, every deed generates a result that contributes to a person's further involvement in or withdrawal from this world. The Hindu tradition recognizes a cycle of rebirth (*samsara*) in which the individual soul (*atman*; see pp.18–19) is repeatedly reincarnated. The actions performed in this life also contribute to an individual's fate in his or her next life. As the *Brihadaranyaka Upanishad* explains, one becomes virtuous by virtuous action, evil by evil action.

Although karma ties a person to the pleasures as well as to the pains of this world, it is believed that the soul ultimately longs to escape from the cycle of rebirth. In the *Bhagavad Gita* (see p.23), Krishna teaches that one cannot simply avoid acting, but one can strive to avoid attachment to actions and their results. Through virtuous living and detachment from the consequences of one's behaviour – that is, by acting disinterestedly, free of egotistical concerns and desire – an individual can advance through a series of lives until he or she reaches spiritual perfection, realizing the final goal of *moksha* and achieving release from *samsara*.

In the Bhagavad Gita, *Krishna observes that the individual soul (*atman*) progresses through the body in infancy, youth and old age, accomplishing many deeds, both glorious and contemptible. At death, the soul simply passes into another body. Krishna explains that while bodies are said to die, the* atman, *which is possessed by the body, is eternal: it cannot be limited or destroyed. Hindus traditionally cremate their dead, and funeral pyres, such as the one shown here on the banks of the Ganges in Varanasi, are commonly found near sacred rivers, where the ashes are scattered after cremation.*

THE FOUR STAGES OF LIFE

Traditional Hindu texts distinguish several stages in the social and spiritual lives of human beings, and rituals have formed to mark the progress of development, from conception to death. Life-cycle sacraments (*samskaras*) begin for a child with ceremonies for such events as naming, first feeding and learning the alphabet. These and other *samskaras* provide forms of education and a process of socialization as young men and women mature and take on more responsibilities within the family and the community. Intended to make a person fit for the next stage of life, each rite involves a degree of reconciliation with certain gods and atonement for sins.

The four major stages of life (*ashramas*) that are traditionally acknowledged for men of the three "twice-born" classes (see below) are those of the student, the householder, the hermit and the ascetic. Special responsibilities (*dharmas*; see p.26) are ascribed to each of these stages. For example, the student is enjoined to study and to serve his guru; while the householder has the specific duty of begetting children. Such responsibilities are codified in treatises, known as *dharma-shastras*, which prescribe duties for every class, caste and stage of life, and also provide guidelines on general moral behaviour. Women's responsibilities (*stridharma*) are usually linked to the dominant male in their lives, whether he is a father, husband or son. In general, women's duties are in service to their families, and they are entrusted with maintaining the health and welfare of their husbands and children.

The *upanayana samskara* initiates a young Hindu into the first stage of life, that of the student (*brahmacarin*). This rite takes place when a boy is between the ages of eight and twelve. Traditionally, a student was required to undergo a rigorous course of study of religious texts under a guru in the guru's house, in preparation for the ritual and social responsibilities that he would be expected to assume as an adult Hindu male. In modern times, the *upanayana* marks a young Hindu's readiness to assume ritual and moral responsibilities, after a much briefer period of study of key sacred texts.

The *ashrama* of concentrated study and celibacy is followed by the householder stage of life, which is initiated by the marriage *samskara* (see p.28). During

Traditionally, boys from the three upper classes – the brahmin, *the* kshatriya *and the* vaishya *(see p.16) – are eligible to undergo the* upanayana samskara. *When they have completed this initiation rite, they are called "twice-born" and may wear a sacred thread, which indicates their status. As part of the ritual, a young boy's head is shaved. The young* brahmin *shown here has had rice grains, symbolizing prosperity, and a* svastika *placed on his head. The* svastika *(which means "creating welfare" in Sanskrit) has been used as an auspicious mark in India since ancient times.*

marriage, a husband and wife are considered partners in *dharma*: together they share ritual and social responsibilities that are centred around bearing and raising children and maintaining the family's welfare. The householder *ashrama* is critical to sustaining the three other *ashramas* (the student, the hermit and the ascetic), all of whom depend on the householder for hospitality and alms.

A man is advised to enter the third stage of life, and become a hermit or forest-dweller (*vanaprastha*), when he sees his first grey hair and lays eyes on a grandchild: these signs indicate that he has completed his social and householder responsibilities. Freed from the duty of maintaining a family, forest-dwellers begin the process of detachment from the material world by simplifying their lives and withdrawing from the bustle of everyday society. This stage prepares an individual for the final *ashrama*: that of the ascetic (*sannyasin*). In this stage, through complete renunciation of all previous attachments and identities, a person's life becomes absorbed in the mystery of understanding the nature of the self and its relationship to the universe.

The schematization of the four stages of life represents an idealized view of the Hindu life-cycle: in reality, few people become hermits or ascetics. Nevertheless, emphasis is still placed on simplicity and on the rewards of non-attachment represented by the last two stages. Many Hindus try to incorporate these virtues into their daily and spiritual lives.

MARRIAGE

The marriage *samskara* (sacrament), known as *vivaha*, while joining two families in a social alliance, also celebrates the union of a man and woman as they enter the householder stage of life. This is one of the most important of all *samskaras* and involves elaborate rituals.

The marriage ceremony takes place after a prolonged period of matchmaking, which includes the consultation of horoscopes in order to fix a date for the wedding as well as to ensure a harmonious and fruitful match between the partners. The ritual of the seven steps (*saptapadi*), which legalizes a marriage, emphasizes the fruits of this partnership, as described in a verse recited by the groom: "One

A Hindu couple walks around the holy fire at their wedding ceremony.

step for sap, two for juice, three for the prospering of wealth, four for comforts, five for cattle, six for seasons. Friend! As you are united with me in this seventh step so may you be devoted to me."

The wife is called "half the husband" (*ardhangi*) and "partner in *dharma*" (*dharmapatni*), and together the husband and wife share the responsibilities of having children, performing certain religious rites and offering hospitality to the needy. Agni, the fire god, is a witness to the vows taken by husband and wife, and during the wedding ceremony grains of rice and clarified butter – symbolic of the prosperity and fertility desired from this union – are offered to him in the sacred fire. The ceremonies culminate with a magnificent wedding feast, during which it is customary for the newly married couple to ladle clarified butter onto the plate of each guest.

THE FOUR AIMS OF LIFE

Hinduism accepts that all human beings have desires and strive for certain goals. In particular, it acknowledges four categories of essential aims that motivate individuals to act and to be involved in the world. These four aims of life (*purusarthas*) are *dharma* (see p.26), the virtuous fulfilment of one's responsibilities; *artha*, material gain, success and wealth; *kama* (see below), pleasure and love; and *moksha* (see pp.30–31), spiritual fulfilment, which is achieved by release from attachment to social, worldly and material aims.

While recognizing that human desires are natural, and that wealth and pleasure can contribute to happiness and well-being, Hindu sages teach that these same desires, when pursued selfishly, can trap a person in a vicious cycle of unhappiness, greed and ignorance. The sacred texts offer advice on how to pursue one's aims in ethically responsible ways, so that one's life is not manipulated by these goals.

It has been suggested that the different stages of life (*ashramas*; see pp.27–8) are particularly conducive to emphasizing one goal over another. The celibate stage of studentship is a good time to pursue *dharma*, because one learns moral and social responsibilities; while marriage and householdership provide a fitting environment for fulfilling the desires for wealth and pleasure, through both material and sexual enjoyments. In the third and fourth stages of life, the impulses for success and pleasure diminish, especially if satisfied during marriage, allowing the individual to become more focused in mind and action on the pursuit of *moksha*. In every stage of life, as well as in the pursuit of all desires and goals, actions are to be governed by *dharma* (righteousness).

KAMA: THE PURSUIT OF PLEASURE

Kama – love or pleasure – although often reduced to an association with sexual pleasure, has a much broader connotation. From the sensuous imagery found in its poetry to the sixteen-fold service of worship that involves all the senses in praise of god, the Hindu tradition draws richly upon the gift of the senses and the pleasures experienced by an individual. *Kama*, explains the *Kama-sutra* composer Vatsyayana, "is the delight of body, mind and soul in exquisite sensation". The pursuit of pleasure is a natural human impulse, which broadens one's experience and knowledge. But the exclusive pursuit of or attachment to pleasure is dangerous, even immoral, leading to greed and suffering and distracting from one's responsibilities and the ultimate goal of *moksha*.

Hinduism recognizes sensual pleasure as a legitimate aim of life. This sculpture, from an 11th-century temple in Khajuraho, shows a couple in an amorous embrace.

PATHS TO SALVATION

*M*oksha (spiritual liberation) is the ultimate goal of a Hindu. True knowledge of the self, explained by some as the identification of one's own soul (*atman*) with the world-soul (*brahman*), brings freedom from attachments, desires and ignorance, as well as from the cycle of rebirth (*samsara*). The quest for salvation has taken many forms, ranging from that of the meditative, reclusive yogi to that of the ecstatic, hymn-singing saint; and Hinduism's acceptance of a variety of spiritual paths underscores its fundamental creed that there is no one way to salvation. Nevertheless, the teachers of the tradition have recognized different methods that can aid a person in the religious pursuit of *moksha*, each suited to different lifestyles and personalities. Three types of spiritual path are outlined as representative of the ways in which human beings seek the divine: these are the paths of knowledge (*jnana-marga*), action (*karma-marga*) and devotion (*bhakti-marga*). All three paths (*margas*), also referred to as disciplines (*yogas*), are commended by Krishna in the *Bhagavad Gita*.

The path of knowledge (*jnana-marga*) is characterized by disciplined study, ethical training and meditation. Meditation often focuses on a particular wisdom passage from a sacred text or on a repeated *mantra*. The premise of this discipline is that ignorance is the cause of human misery and separation from *brahman*; knowledge liberates people from the boundaries of the ego and its perceived finitude. Most begin the journey along the path of knowledge under the guidance of a guru (teacher), by contemplating the nature of the self. What is

The 15th-century Bengali saint Caitanya, shown in this modern poster, characterizes the bhakti *(devotional) path to salvation with his wholehearted commitment to Krishna.*

sought is not merely an intellectual understanding of the self, but intuitive wisdom that will lead to first-hand knowledge of the individual soul's identity with the universal soul. This meditation requires great physical and mental discipline, including the restraint of the senses, and is particularly suited to a reclusive and ascetic lifestyle. The student, forest-dweller and renunciant stages of life (see pp.27–8) provide an environment that is supportive to this path, because during these times a person is freed from social responsibilities and may concentrate on the restraint and purification of both mind and body.

The path of action (*karma-marga*) is driven by the selfless performance of one's designated duties and obligations (*svadharma*) in the world. The path presumes that the rewards of one's labours compel an individual to act. However, because these rewards are temporary, they trap a person in a cycle: one works to realize a particular desire, only to be disappointed when the experience or novelty of that pleasure wears out. Desire motivates action, but this same desire eventually brings pain and disappointment – in turn, binding a person to the cycle of rebirth.

To attain *moksha* while remaining active in the world, a person must be unattached to the outcomes of his or her actions. One may perform one's prescribed responsibilities selflessly, for the sake of the world; or one may act in the name of god, dedicating one's service and the fruits of one's actions to god. In either case, a person's involvement in the world becomes a conscious spiritual discipline. Dedicated service, selfless work, great discipline, humility and

SPIRITUAL YOGA AND THE *YOGA SUTRA*

The word "yoga" has been used in India to refer to many types of disciplined activity beyond the familiar system of exercises properly known as Hatha Yoga. As a general term it has been applied to broad paths of spiritual growth, as in the *Bhagavad Gita* (see p.23), which speaks of the *yogas* of knowledge, action and devotion (see left). As a more specific term, it refers to the classical system of philosophy outlined in the *Yoga Sutra*, an early text attributed to the sage Patanjali, which proposes mental concentration as a path to spiritual liberation.

The *Yoga Sutra* relies on the school of Sankhya philosophy, which describes the evolution of the world in a series of stages. The self of each individual is in its true nature a separate entity, distinct from all manifestations of physical matter. During the course of evolution, however, the ego develops through attachments to material objects. The yoga school teaches the practitioner how to reverse this process of evolution by exercising increasingly subtle and powerful forms of control so as to move the awareness of the self away from an entanglement with worldly objects. The *Yoga Sutra* describes stages of accomplishment – such as levitation and clairvoyance

Visual objects, such as this 18th-century bronze yantra *(a meditational aid), provide one means of focusing the mind in yoga.*

– but warns that these can be dangerous sidetracks. The ultimate goal is not to gain power within the world, but to gain the power of escaping from the world altogether, and moving beyond the necessity of rebirth.

obedience are characteristic of the saintly men and women who pursue this difficult path of being in the world but not of the world.

For those who follow the path of devotion (*bhakti-marga*), whether their lives are characterized by renunciation or by social commitment, *moksha* involves a complete surrender to god. In the *Bhagavad Gita* (see p.23), Krishna reveals himself to be the supreme deity, who assumes a human form so that he can enter into a personal relationship with humans. The path of *bhakti* is characterized by this personal relationship with god: individuals achieve liberation through the grace and direct personal

experience of god. The accessibility and personality of god account for the popularity of the *bhakti* path to salvation. No special knowledge, language or ritual is required to relate to god on a personal level.

Of the three main paths to salvation, *karma-marga* is characterized by dedicating one's works and service to god, *jnana-marga* by concentrating one's mind and thoughts on knowing the true self, and *bhakti-marga* by coming to know and experience god through the emotions and senses. Although each path has a distinct orientation, none is exclusive. Many Hindus draw from several disciplines as they individualize their spiritual path and practice.

MANIFESTATIONS OF THE DIVINE

From the reverence for Mother Earth to the honouring of the sacred cow (see below), Hindus have long recognized the sanctity of nature. The Vedic gods of the Aryans possessed powers that were associated with the elements of nature; and the Rig Veda is filled with hymns that praise and appease these divinities. Each of the important natural forces – fire, earth, wind, atmosphere and sky – was represented by an individual deity, led by the heroic Indra, god of thunder. Different deities are still believed to preside over different seasons, months and days of the year: Shiva, with the crescent moon in his hair, is the guardian of Monday, and Surya, the sun god, presides over Sunday. Although the Hindu tradition recognizes a multiplicity of gods, all are often considered to be manifestations of the one ultimate god, conceived of as *brahman* (see pp.18–19).

In Hindu thought, divinity is a natural part of this world, not separate from it. It exists in rocks and rivers, mountains and caves, plants and trees. Other natural forms are worshipped as spontaneous manifestations of the divine. Certain plants are revered because they are associated with a particular deity. For example, the *tulasi* (sacred basil plant) is identified with Vishnu, and is believed to be dear to his avatar Krishna: the prayer beads of Vishnu devotees

THE SACRED COW

The cow has long been venerated by Hindus and is identified with Mother Earth: both are sources of food and fuel, as well as of fertilizer. Because the sacred cow is said to be an embodiment of the benevolence of the gods, depictions of her often show different deities residing in different parts of her body. A valued commodity, the cow is one of the most precious gifts that can be given in the context of a Hindu religious ceremony: the wealth of a ritual's patron is often assessed by the number of cows presented. The five products (*pancagavya*) of the cow – milk, curd, butter, urine and dung – are used in religious ceremonies and are believed to

In Nepal, cows are especially worshipped on the festival day of Gai Yatra, when they are decorated and presented with food and coins.

have purifying properties.

The cow symbolizes prosperity and fertility, and throughout India cows wander the streets freely, revered and cared for by the Hindus whose paths they cross. In a gesture of both devotion and respect, Hindus will touch the shank or forehead of a cow and utter a prayer, hoping that the cow will grant all their wishes.

Women draw hoof-prints of the cow at the thresholds of their homes as an auspicious sign of blessing to everyone who enters. And periodic festivals are held to honour all sorts of bovines, including the milk-producing water buffaloes and the plough-pulling Brahma bulls.

ABOVE *A shrine stands at the base of a sacred banyan tree, which is revered as a symbol of longevity and regeneration.*

RIGHT *The Ganges River, visited by thousands of pilgrims, is believed to wash away not only the dust of the road but also the sins of the day.*

are often made from wood of the *tulasi*. Throughout India, planters full of *tulasi* grace the courtyards of Hindu homes, and women of the household worship and water this symbol of Vishnu daily.

Water is a source of divinity in Hinduism, because it purifies and nourishes. At the end of a given cosmic cycle (see p.25), after the world has been destroyed by flames, everything is absorbed into the ocean of dissolution, from which the process of re-creation begins. Rivers are sacred because they descend from the heavens to purify and fertilize the earth. Unusual or spectacular natural phenomena, such as fords of rivers and crevices in mountains, are identified as *tirthas* (fords or crossings; see p.46), where the presence of the sacred is especially intense. In these places, cosmic and historical time intersect and the distinction between the transcendent and the mundane is blurred, giving individuals a glimpse of the purity and the blissful nature of the divine.

The divine also manifests itself within the human imagination, giving rise to a plethora of anthropomorphic images in Hinduism. Many deities are depicted with multiple arms or heads, symbolic

of their superhuman powers. The triad of deities (*trimurti*) representing the powers of creation, preservation and destruction are Brahma, Vishnu and Shiva. Brahma, his four heads denoting the four Vedas, controls the process of creation. Vishnu, in his ten incarnations (avatars), defeats the threat of *adharma* (evil) and re-establishes order in the universe. Shiva's role as destroyer is suggested by his white complexion powdered with ashes from the cremation fire; yet even in his meditative state he has an erect penis, symbol of the cycle of regeneration that follows the process of destruction.

Everything is touched by the sacred, even the demonic beings of Hindu mythology. These demons are blessed with superhuman powers but cursed with subhuman personalities, symbolized by their grotesque features. Evil is recognized as a part of nature that can cause havoc in the world of humans and gods; the goal is to overcome it with righteous, *dharmic* behaviour. However, the battle between *dharma* and *adharma* is not easy, especially during the dismal Kali Yuga (the current age; see p.25), when morality is at its lowest.

VISHNU AND HIS AVATARS

Vishnu, one of the most popular Hindu deities, is the preserver who protects and sustains this world. He is depicted in art as a handsome, four-armed man, whose erect posture and crown distinguish him as a righteous king. In each of his four hands, he carries a different symbol: a mace, token of his royal power; a discus, the invincible weapon presented to him by Indra, king of the gods; a lotus, representing his part in creation (see p.25); and a conch, which sounds his victory over disorder. The discus and the conch are the most common symbols of Vishnu and are used as motifs in temples and homes where Vishnu's presence is invoked.

This 18th-century painting from Bundi, India, shows Vishnu and his consort Lakshmi, riding on Garuda, Vishnu's devoted, eagle-like mount who represents valour.

As the preserver of universal order, Vishnu is often required to descend to earth to defeat evil and restore harmony, saving humans from their own wickedness. The mythology of Vishnu tells of ten different avatars (incarnations). The best-known of these are Krishna (see p.36) and Rama (see p.37), and devotion to Vishnu most often takes the form of the worship of one of these two divine heroes, along with their respective consorts, Radha and Sita.

In his first four descents to earth, Vishnu assumed animal or part-animal forms. As Matsya, he appeared as a fish to save both humankind and the Vedas from the great flood that came about in an era soon after creation. As Kurma, a tortoise, Vishnu played a role in the churning of the milk ocean from which the world emerged, according to one Hindu creation myth (see p.25). As Varaha, a boar, he again rescued the earth from a deluge of waters.

The story of Vishnu's fourth descent, as the man-lion Narasimha, involves a king who was given the gift of conditional immortality by Shiva: he could not be killed either by a man or by a beast, during the day or at night, or inside or outside his palace. Confident in his immortality, the king became a tyrant and forbade his son to worship Vishnu. The god put an end to the king's arrogance by taking the form of a man-lion (neither man nor beast), approaching him at dusk (neither day nor night) and tearing out his intestines on the verandah of his palace (neither inside nor out).

In his fifth descent, Vishnu came to earth as a dwarf, Vamana, at a time when the demon king Bali had disrupted the order of the world to such an extent that the gods were powerless against him. Having been granted the gift of as much land as he could tread in three steps, the dwarf transformed himself into a giant and used his three steps to gain control of the underworld, the earth and the heavens, vanquishing the demon king. Parashurama, the sixth avatar, was a martial hero who avenged the death of his *brahmin* father at the hands of a *kshatriya* warrior and restored the *brahmin* orthodoxy to its place of superiority. Rama, the seventh avatar, defeated the demon Ravana, a symbol of the powers of evil that pervade the world (see p.22); and Krishna, the eighth avatar, righted many wrongs and brought joy and love into the world.

In contrast to the first eight avatars, the ninth descent of Vishnu, the Buddha, is a figure of recent historical times. Like Vishnu, the Buddha is seen as

a saviour who, through teaching and example, helped direct humanity toward the right path of living. The tenth avatar of Vishnu has yet to appear. It is predicted that Kalki will arrive on a white horse (or as a horse himself), heralding the end of the present era, the Kali Yuga (see p.25).

In addition to the ten avatars, numerous other manifestations of Vishnu are recognized in the temples and myths of different Indian regions. In the state of Maharashtra, in western India, the most popular form of Vaishnava devotion is directed to Vithoba, whose main shrine is in Pandharpur (see map, p.17). In Tirupati (see map, p.17), the site of the wealthiest and perhaps most-visited temple in India, Vishnu is worshipped as Venkateshvara.

In almost all depictions of Vishnu, his consort Lakshmi is at his side. The goddess of wealth and good fortune, she is worshipped in her own right as Mahalakshmi. Born from the churning of the ocean, she is shown seated on a lotus, symbolic of creation and of her pure beauty. This royal couple, familiarly known as Shri Vishnu and Lakshmi-Narayana, embody the virtues of generosity and mercy, while overseeing and protecting the order of creation.

KRISHNA

A bronze relief from the City Palace in Jaipur shows Krishna and his beloved gopi *Radha. The loving relationship between Krishna and Radha symbolizes the intimate union with god that Krishna offers.*

Krishna is perhaps the most dynamic and beloved of Vishnu's avatars, the embodiment of divinity and of divine love. Stories about him and the different episodes in his life abound in Hindu texts and folklore. In the *Mahabharata* (see p.23) he is the charioteer and adviser to Arjuna; and in the *Bhagavad Gita* (see p.23), he reveals his true nature as the supreme god, the ultimate reality that is all things.

According to legend, Krishna was raised by foster parents in Brindavan (see map, p.17), a pastoral community in northern India. He was a charming and precocious but mischievous child, whose extraordinary strength and startling miracles proved that he was indeed an embodiment of divinity. On one occasion his foster mother, Yashoda, scolded him for eating mud and insisted that he open his mouth for inspection. When he did so, she was astounded to see the whole universe contained within. Krishna revealed to her his true nature: he himself was the earth that he had eaten; there was no distinction. Another story depicts Krishna dancing on the head

of the serpent king, Kaliya, who was poisoning the water with his venom. Despite being bitten by the serpent and squeezed in its muscular coils, Krishna freed himself and subdued his foe. This feat suggests that people who worship Krishna will also be freed from the fetters that bind them.

Krishna's protection of his devotees derives from his love for them, a theme popularly expressed in the story of his seduction of the cowherd women (*gopis*). Lured to the forest by the enchanting call of Krishna's flute (representing the voice of god), the *gopis* were consumed by their passion for Krishna. Krishna demonstrated the infinite nature of his love by appearing to dance with them individually. As each *gopi* experienced the personal attention of Krishna, so each devotee, focusing his or her worship solely on Lord Krishna, enters into an intimate union with god. The worship of Krishna is illustrative of the path of *bhakti* (devotion) in which *moksha* (release; see pp.30–31) is attained by surrendering to the power of god's love.

RAMA AND SITA

The name of Rama is on the lips of many Hindus as they rise in the mornings, as they pray and even as they take their final breaths: *"Ram, Ram"* is a common greeting throughout India, and when carrying a corpse to the cremation ground, mourners chant *"Ram-nam satya hai"* (the name of god [alone] is real). To recite the name of Rama, hero of the *Ramayana* (see p.22) and seventh avatar of the supreme Lord Vishnu, is one way for Hindus to partake of the experience of the divine and to acquire great spiritual merit.

The *Ramayana* presents Rama as the ideal man and his wife, Sita, as the paragon of womanhood. Hindus long for the return of the Golden Age in which Rama reigned, when righteousness (*dharma*) flourished. The perfect man,

This miniature painting shows Rama being worshipped by his trusted servant Hanuman, the monkey god, while Sita and Lakshmana (Rama's brother) look on.

Rama is an obedient son, a conscientious ruler and a loving husband; being of the *kshatriya* class, he is also a heroic warrior, who defeats the demon Ravana, abductor of his wife. Sita, the model woman, is devoted to her husband: she accompanies him in his exile and later undergoes a fire ordeal to prove her innocence and loyalty.

Together, Rama and Sita portray the ideal of conjugal love, representing the totality of the godhead as beneficent champions of universal harmony. When Hindus call out *"Ram, Ram"*, or chant *"Ram-Sita-Ram"* as they bathe in the Ganges River, they are invoking the forces of goodness, righteousness and morality – embodied in Rama – to guide and inspire their lives, leading them on the path to perfection.

HANUMAN, THE MONKEY GOD

Hanuman, the trusted general of the monkey army, whose deeds are celebrated in the *Ramayana*, represents the ideal *bhakta* (devotee), who serves his master with unquestioning loyalty and obedience. By fulfilling Rama's every need and wish, he himself was fulfilled and achieved great spiritual freedom.

Hanuman's humility and service provide a spiritual model for many Hindus, and he is also respected for

his considerable knowledge. Because of the healing herb he administered to save the lives of Rama and Lakshmana when they were mortally wounded in battle, his blessings are sought for protection and good health, especially of children. Son of Vayu, the wind god, he is as swift as the wind, and his athletic abilities have made him the patron deity of weightlifters and wrestlers.

SHIVA

Shiva is part of the central Hindu triad (*trimurti*) of Brahma, Vishnu and Shiva, which represents the cosmic processes of creation, sustenance and destruction. As such, he is Shiva the destroyer. However, Shiva is also a power of re-creation and fertility. In having one figure simultaneously embody the seemingly opposite traits of destruction and re-creation, Hinduism acknowledges the natural and interconnected processes of birth, death and rebirth.

The origins of Shiva worship, and its connection with fertility, may date at least from Vedic times. Shiva has been associated with the Vedic deity Rudra and compared to the pre-Aryan Lord of Animals, who with his yogic posture, long tresses and erect penis is known as the proto-Shiva. Shiva has many epithets, such as Sadashiva, Shankara and Shambhu, but he is best known as Mahadeva (the greatest of gods) or Maheshvara (Great Lord). He is often represented in art with matted hair, symbolic of his ascetism; a stream of water flowing from his head, indicating his role in facilitating the sacred river Ganges' descent from the heavens; a garland

This Shiva linga, *set in a* yoni, *stands in the courtyard of a temple in Bhubaneshwar. The offerings of red bilva leaves and white jasmine are thought to be favoured by Shiva.*

and girdle of serpents; and a trident, the most significant of his weapons. He derived his blue throat from drinking a poison that threatened the future of the world, an act that illustrates the compassionate side of his nature.

Shiva's ambivalent personality manifests the extremes of asceticism and eroticism. As an ascetic, he is often depicted in deep meditation, either on Mount Kailasa, his heavenly abode, or in a cremation ground, where he sits naked, covered with ashes and garlanded with snakes. From this intense meditation, which can last thousands of years, comes Shiva's great wisdom and power, symbolized by his third eye. The fiery energy (*tejas*) amassed by his austerities can be emitted in a blink of this eye, bringing about either destruction or enlightenment.

Shiva's great asceticism allows him to contain as well as to control his sexual energies, and this balance of ascetic discipline and creative force is represented by portraits of him sitting in meditation with an erect penis. He is the erotic ascetic: his extraordinary control during intercourse enabled him to make love to his wife, Parvati, for hundreds of years without ever emitting his seed.

Shiva represents the cosmic energy of the universe, and in his various forms he channels that force toward different ends. As Nataraja (see p.40), he exerts himself in dance, controlling the rhythm of the universe; as Bhairava, the Terrible, he represents the unconventional that springs from passion and impulse; and as Dakshinamurti, the yogi and guru, he directs his energy toward teaching. Shiva is most commonly worshipped through the *linga*, a form symbolic of the phallus. The *linga* protrudes from a *yoni*, which represents the vulva and female energy, and together the two signify the union of male and female and the totality of existence. In temples, water

A modern street poster from Bombay depicts the "divine family" of Shiva, Parvati and Ganesha (see p.41). Shiva is the aloof ascetic figure of the male god, while Parvati is the female embodiment of his shakti *(divine energy), and as such can more readily be invoked to act in human affairs. The benign manifestation of Shiva's consort, Parvati is associated with goodness, benevolence, fidelity and abundance. Shiva and Parvati represent the union of the masculine and feminine, the opposite principles which – like birth and death, light and darkness – are ultimately inter-connected and indivisible. Their oneness and omnipotence is illustrated in a story in which Ganesha was challenged to circle the whole world, and did so by circling his parents.*

from a pot often drips over the *linga* to cool the fiery energy that it represents. Outside the threshold of a Shiva temple, looking inward at his lord, is a statue of Nandi, the bull who is Shiva's mount. Nandi is both guardian and devotee of Shiva, and, like his master, he is widely worshipped as a symbol of fertility and strength.

The *Linga Purana* explains the worship of the Shiva *linga* with the following myth. One day Brahma and Vishnu were arguing about who was the creator of the world (each wanting to claim this divine act as his own), when suddenly a luminous shaft of light appeared before them. Seeing no end or beginning to this fiery pillar, the two gods set out to investigate the phenomenon. Brahma assumed the form of a goose and flew up in search of the top of the shaft, while Vishnu turned himself into a boar and started digging to find its root. Failing to discover the source of the light, they bowed before it to honour this superior force – at this moment, Shiva appeared before them in all his glorious radiance. Revealing that this pillar of light (*jyotirlinga*) was a manifestation of his own special form, Shiva informed Brahma and Vishnu that they were both born from him; and thereby he asserted his dominant place as creator of the universe.

When not alone in meditation or leading his followers into battle, Shiva is accompanied by his wife

Parvati, daughter of the mountain Himalaya. In different episodes that span many lifetimes, Parvati appears in various forms. As Uma, Sati and Gauri, she is the benign companion of Shiva. However, as Mahadevi, the Great Goddess, she exhibits a different and more dynamic personality; and as Kali and Durga (see pp.42–3), she appears in ferocious, destructive forms. The "divine family" of Parvati and Shiva includes Skanda (born when Shiva's semen fell into the river Ganges) and Ganesha (created from the skin of Parvati; see p.41). Together, Shiva and Parvati represent the complementary and dynamic nature of Shiva-*shakti*, the primordial principles of energy and matter that give rise to creation. Shiva represents the creative potency that is inherent in the universe and in each individual. In worshipping Shiva, devotees access the well of potency that makes all things possible.

THE DANCING SHIVA

One of the best-known representations of Shiva is that of Nataraja, Lord of the Dance. This dynamic depiction presents Shiva as the creative energy of the universe, which gives life and protects it, but also takes it away.

As Nataraja, Shiva holds a drum in his upper right hand: this beats steadily as the heartbeat of life, representing the rhythm of creation. In his upper left hand, he holds a flame from which the destruction of the world by fire begins. The circle of flames that envelops Shiva portrays the continual cycle of destruction and renewal of life (see p.24), which is activated by the creative energy of Shiva: when Shiva's cosmic dance comes to an end, so too does the world. However, the dance always begins again, initiating the process of re-creation. Shiva's dance also symbolizes the destruction of ignorance and evil, denoted by the dwarf whom he tramples underfoot.

Despite his power to destroy, Shiva also seeks to protect the world and his devotees. His forward right hand is raised in a gesture (*mudra*) that means "Do not fear", while his forward left hand points down to his raised foot, signalling that all who approach him with devotion may find protection at his feet.

The Nataraja image brilliantly illustrates both the calm and the flux that exist in the world. The face of this cosmic dancer is impassive, serene and at peace, while the rest of his body twirls and swirls in response to the flow of energy that moves the world.

This 11th-century bronze statue from southern India depicts Shiva Nataraja dancing in the circle of fire. Shiva's dance is a clear symbol of the unity of existence and the dynamic rhythm of both destructive and creative processes at work in the universe.

GANESHA

*Ganesha, whose presence is invoked at all auspicious ceremonies, is depicted in
this wall-painting on the side of a wedding hall in Jaisalmer, Rajasthan.*

Ganesha, the popular elephant-headed deity, is known as the Remover of Obstacles and Lord of Beginnings. He is a member of the "divine family" that also comprises his so-called father Shiva, his mother Parvati and his brother Skanda (see p.40).

The most common account of Ganesha's birth explains how he acquired his unusual head. While Parvati was bathing one day she formed a young man from the dirt and sweat that she scrubbed off her leg. Giving life to the figure (who later came to be known as Ganesha), she asked him to stand guard at the door to her bath and let no one in. Her husband, Shiva, who had been away when Ganesha was created, arrived home and insisted on seeing his wife. He and the young man standing guard came to blows, neither of them aware of the other's relationship to Parvati. In the course of this fight, Shiva cut off Ganesha's head, only to find that he had killed Parvati's son. Parvati insisted that Ganesha's life be restored, and Shiva ordered one of his retinue to go out and bring back the head of the first creature he saw: this was an elephant. Placing the head on Ganesha's shoulders, Shiva brought him back to life.

Ganesha is greatly revered for his wisdom and courage, and as the Remover of Obstacles and Lord of Beginnings he is invoked at the beginning of every ceremony and before any new undertaking, especially before a journey or a new project. Weddings and other beginnings are blessed by him, including the new year. Images of Ganesha are found above the thresholds of homes, at the top of wedding invitations and at the entrances to temples.

Ganesha is known to put up obstacles as well as to remove them, but he is generally a congenial deity, popular for his cunning and lighthearted trickery. His vehicle is the sly rat, who, like many of Ganesha's devotees, is eager to taste the sweetness of life. Ganesha's enormous belly symbolizes his embodiment of a successful and prosperous life, and he is usually depicted with a bowl of sweets. His left tusk is broken off because, according to legend, he used it as a pen to transcribe the *Mahabharata* (see p.23) when Vyasa dictated it to him. In recent times, the wise and convivial Ganesha has become a patron saint of students, who pray to him fervently for help in passing their exams.

THE GODDESS

*In this early 18th-century painting, Durga is shown defeating the demon armies with
the help of Kali, "the black one", a manifestation of the Goddess who emanates
from Durga's anger and delights in the blood of the battlefield.*

The worship of Devi, the Goddess, is prevalent throughout India, and archaeological evidence from the Indus Valley civilizations suggests that the worship of the female in India is extremely ancient and may even be indigenous to the area. The cult of the mother or female fertility symbol was probably eclipsed by the Aryans, whose sacred texts were dominated by such male divinities as Indra, Rudra and Varuna. However, the very power (*shakti*) of these gods later emerged as one of the most powerful aspects of the Goddess.

In the Vedas *shakti* refers to the divine powers displayed by each of the gods; later it came to refer to the potential energy of the gods, the internal force that causes them to act and primordial matter to evolve. This creative, dynamic force was

*In wayside shrines, the Goddess is
represented by rounded stones, such
as the one above. The stones are
anointed with red powder, symbolic
of fertility, auspiciousness and life.*

conceived of as female, and by the time of the *Puranas* (*c.*4th–10th centuries CE) goddesses (*devis*) had appeared alongside the Hindu male deities as external manifestations of their power or strength. For example, Sarasvati, goddess of learning and wisdom, is the consort of Brahma, the creator god; Lakshmi (see p.35), goddess of wealth and good fortune, stands alongside Vishnu, preserver of the universe; and Parvati (see p.40), in her many manifestations, represents the *shakti* of Shiva, who without her presence would remain inert.

The worship of *shakti* as represented by these *devis* developed into a separate cult, and the Goddess is envisioned simultaneously as the creator, sustainer and destroyer of the universe. One myth tells of her conquest of the buffalo-demon

Mahisa, who had taken over the heavens and the earth. In this story, the goddess Durga is created from the splendour of several of the great male deities, after they have shown themselves to be unable to defeat Mahisa. Armed with weapons presented to her by each of the gods and aided by the bloodthirsty Kali, Durga defeats Mahisa's armies, saving both gods and humans from this embodiment of evil. In the *Devi-Mahatmya*, a well-known Hindu text, the gods praise Devi as the mother of the universe, and describe her as the remover of all suffering, fear and evil; it is she who will bring everyone to final liberation. Devi, in turn, promises to protect those who remember her and come to her for refuge.

The Goddess is generally identified with one of her numerous manifestations, and each village in India seems to be blessed by its own local *devi*. However, while each of these local goddesses may have her own name and be associated with a particular myth or power, all are encompassed in the idea of Mahadevi, the Great Goddess.

The individual manifestations of the Great Goddess represent her different personalities. Some, such as Sarasvati and Lakshmi, are benevolent, compassionate and nurturing, providing their devotees with wisdom, wealth, food, good health and long life. In these goddesses the female is associated with fertility and prosperity. Others, such as Kali and Chinnamasta, who are frequently depicted drinking blood, represent a much more frightening aspect. Some Hindus believe that epidemics are the results of the Goddess' wrath at being neglected. Devi reminds her devotees that just as she can be a giver of life and abundance, so too can she take away these gifts. Invariably, however, she is concerned with the well-being of her devoted children, and in both her benign and terrifying forms, she is considered an approachable listener to the prayers of her devotees.

While the Goddess is often worshipped in the form of a woman (albeit sometimes with multiple heads and arms), she is also revered in other forms. In Shiva temples, she is represented by the *yoni*, a stylized vulva, from which the Shiva *linga* (see pp.38–9) protrudes. The Goddess is also depicted by certain geometric shapes, notably the triangle, which symbolizes the vulva, the seat of a woman's sexuality. Like such gods as Vishnu, Shiva and Ganesha, each of whom travels on his own particular mount, the various manifestations of the Goddess have animal mounts. Sarasvati is shown with a goose or peacock; Durga rides a lion; and Mahalakshmi is flanked by elephants. The trident and the lotus, two symbols that are traditionally associated with Shiva and Vishnu, respectively, often appear in connection with the Goddess; the trident denotes her ability to both protect and destroy, the lotus her ability to create.

A clay image of Sarasvati, the goddess of learning and the arts, who is worshipped by students, poets and musicians.

43

TEMPLES AND SHRINES

The Hindu religious tradition is rich with stories about gods and goddesses who manifest themselves on earth in order to make themselves and their powers more accessible to humans. Hindu temples are the earthly homes of these gods, who otherwise dwell in the heavens. Some temples are built at particular sites to commemorate, capture and intensify the active intersection of the human and the divine; others are built as invitations to the divine.

Hindu temples are places of retreat where a devotee can focus his or her prayers and meditations. They range from the smallest and simplest wayside shrines (see below) to elaborate temple complexes, which operate like small-scale cities. The architectural shape of many temples resembles a mountain, modelled on Mount Kailasa, the sacred abode of

Shiva, or on Mount Meru, which is at the centre of the universe, according to Hindu mythology. Entering such a temple is like entering a cavern in a mountain: there is little natural light. One progresses through a series of dim antechambers to the *garbha-griha* (womb) of the temple, where the main deity resides. This holiest of places is vertically aligned with the highest point of the temple, the *shikhara* (peak or crest).

Two types of classical temple architecture prevail in India, generally known as the northern and southern schools, although there are many regional variations. Northern-style temples are characterized by a series of spires (*shikharas*), resembling hills and mountains, with the highest located over the main sanctuary. The temples at Sanchi, Bhubaneshwar,

WAYSIDE SHRINES

The wayside shrines and small temples that dot the Indian countryside stand in sharp contrast to the great temples that draw pilgrims from all over the country. Found beneath trees, in fields of corn, at fords in streams, on mountain pathways and even beneath street lamps at urban intersections, these small shrines are reminders of the sacredness of the everyday.

Wayside shrines are often established by a single devotee who has undergone a mystical experience at the particular site. Usually made from local materials, such as clay, bamboo, straw or stone, these informal shrines house a variety of images, such as a geometric design symbolic of the Goddess or a bas-relief of two entwined snakes, representing the *nagas*, which are associated with fertility and are often worshipped by women who desire to have children. Wayside shrines

A devotee stops at a wayside Shiva shrine, which stands along the Brahmaputra River. Outside the shrine are smaller shrines to Hanuman (far left) and the nagas.

invite spontaneous communication with the divine, and passersby may utter a prayer, stop briefly to offer a flower, or even delay their journey to perform a more elaborate worship.

The 11th-century Vishnavatha temple (dedicated to Shiva) at Khajuraho, in the state of Madhya Pradesh, is an example of the classical northern style of Hindu temple architecture. Like many of the temples at Khajuraho, it is adorned with erotic sculpture.

Puri and Khajuraho, along with the cave temples at Ellora and Elephanta, offer some excellent examples of the northern style from different regions and historical periods. In the south, the temple complex is surrounded by a courtyard that is entered through one of several towered gateways (*gopurams*). Like the tower that rises over the main sanctuary, they are elaborately carved with details related to the powers and feats of the deity to whom the temple is dedicated. The monolithic temples at Mahabalipuram in Karnataka present a range of different architectural forms found in many southern-style temples; those at Kanchipuram, along with the Minakshi temple in Madurai, represent the exquisite detail of southern

Indian religious architecture. In both schools, great attention is given to the placement and orientation of the temple: most are built on an east–west axis, with the shrine of the main deity in the east, and the main entrance in the west.

The Hindu temple is not designed for communal worship, although the outer courtyards are often used for special festivals. Most pilgrims come to the temple to experience god through *darshana*, the viewing of the holy image of the deity. Pilgrims must purify themselves before entering the temple precinct by performing ablutions and removing their shoes. A pilgrim will often approach the subsidiary shrines of attendants of the main deity to implore their blessings before approaching the sanctuary where the essence of god is contained. A devotee may come to ask a special favour, to fulfil a vow or to partake of the *prasada* (grace of god), which is symbolized by the food offered to the god during worship and then distributed to the faithful. Only the ritual priests who attend the deity are allowed within the inner sanctuary, where the image of the god resides; most Hindus gaze upon the deity from outside this sanctuary, where they prostrate themselves in prayer and humility. To make sure that they have appealed to and honoured all aspects of the god, pilgrims perform a ritual of circumambulation of the deity, stopping at each of the cardinal directions to touch their hands or foreheads to the wall surrounding the sanctuary.

The classically styled temples combine the most beautiful aspects of Indian architecture and sculpture: gateways, towers and walls are carved with mythological figures and events. On the threshold, sculptures of guardian deities threaten any demonic forces that might defile the sacred space; and in various niches throughout the temple, symbols of prosperity and auspiciousness abound, such as the lotus, the banyan tree, the *svastika* and intertwined lovers. Such religious motifs edify the pilgrim and reinforce his or her spiritual experience.

PILGRIMAGE AND RELIGIOUS DEVOTION

Images of the deities are bathed with holy water during the anniversary celebration of the Kapalisvara temple, Madras. A pilgrim may sponsor a bathing ritual and accrue merit.

Almost every mountain, river and plain in India has special significance in the religious imagination of Hindus. These sacred sites are called *tirthas* (fords or crossings), as they are believed to be places where people can cross over from the mundane concerns of life to an experience of transcendence. Many *tirthas* are associated with particular gods, heroes and saints, and shrines are built at these locations to capture and to commemorate the divine presence. Pilgrims approach with reverence and humility, arriving by boat, bus, moped, bicycle, on foot or even on their knees. Most pilgrims come to take *darshana* – to experience the grace and love of god through seeing and being seen by the image of god.

The religious devotions conducted at pilgrimage sites are similar to those observed by Hindus in their homes and local temples. In *puja* (the ritual worship of god) the deity is treated like an honoured guest: invited to inhabit its image, the god is offered water, fresh clothing, a seat of honour, a meal and other comforts. At the conclusion of *puja*, a worshipper partakes of *prasada* (literally, god's grace), in the form of a food offering that has been enjoyed by the god and is then shared with the devotee.

Most pilgrimage centres are dedicated to particular deities. For example, the *shakta-pithas* found throughout southern Asia are centres of the Goddess: each one is associated with a certain part of Sati's body, which was dismembered by Vishnu after the goddess' death in order to assuage the grief of her husband, Shiva. Lesser pilgrimage sites include those known as "Sita's Kitchens", which are deemed sacred because Sita and Rama are said to have camped there during their years in exile (see p.22).

Pilgrimage routes can be regional and specialized, such as the circuit of the *Astavinayakas*, eight natural manifestations of Ganesha found in the state of Maharashtra. Others routes are popular among particular sects. The twelve *lingas* of light (*jyotirlingas*; see p.39) of Shiva are sacred to Shaivas; and the towns of Mathura, Brindavan and Dwaraka (see map, p.17) are visited by Vaishnavas because of their association with the life of Krishna, Vishnu's avatar.

Many sacred centres are visited by pilgrims from all regions and sects. The Himalayas are the mythological home of Shiva, and these mighty mountains also contain the source of the holy river Ganges, which breaks its fall from heaven in the dreadlocks of Shiva's hair, before blessing the thirsty plains with its nurturing waters. Hardwar, the town where the Ganges emerges from the Himalayas, draws pilgrims from all over India; and Gangotri, Kedarnath and Badrinath have developed at the sources of the Ganges' three branches. Varanasi, also known as Benares or Kashi (the city of light), is another site that is blessed by the Ganges and sacred to Shiva. Considered to be the holiest of Indian cities,

Pilgrims arriving by boat at Varanasi on the river Ganges. Thousands of people travel to this sacred city each year to immerse themselves in the holy river, often taking home vials of river water to keep on the family altar.

Varanasi draws thousands of pilgrims yearly, many of whom bring the ashes of a relative to sprinkle in the holy river. Other pilgrims travel to Varanasi to await their own deaths, because this city and this river, with their heightened sanctity, are considered *mokshadvaras* (doors to liberation).

Numerous *tirthas* in India confer merit on those who approach with a pure mind and heart. The *Mahabharata* mentions seven particular holy cities (Varanasi, Mathura, Ujjain, Hardwar, Prayag, Ayodhya and Gaya), and thousands flock to these sacred centres in northern India in search of spiritual merit and purification. There are also sites of great sanctity in the south, including Rameshwaram, made holy by Rama's bath of atonement; Madurai, the central place of worship of the goddess Minakshi; Kanchipuram, known as the "Varanasi of the South", with its 124 temples; Tirupati, home of the wealthiest temple in India, dedicated to Vishnu; and Shrirangam, centre of Shri Vaishnava devotions.

In the Hindu imagination, the subcontinent of India is conceived of as *Jambu-dvipa* (rose-apple island) or *Bharata Mata* (Mother India). In each of the four cardinal directions, an elephant stands guard over this sacred land. The belief in *Bharata* as both holy land and mother land has fostered a sense of solidarity that transcends regional, linguistic and sectarian differences. To traverse India via its cardinal *tirthas* – Badrinath in the north, Puri in the east, Rameshwaram in the south and Dwaraka in the west (see map, p.17) – is considered equal to circling the earth, and brings exceptional merit. The practice of pilgrimage, which can lead a Hindu to many different regions of India while tracing sacred history, has in many ways contributed to a sense of national unity.

OVERLEAF Sadhus *(religious mendicants) gather in Allahabad (also known as Prayag), at the confluence of the holy Ganges and Yamuna rivers, during the Kumbha-mela festival (see pp.50–51). Pilgrims also regularly visit the sacred city of Allahabad to take a ritual bath.*

FESTIVALS AND HOLY DAYS

Worshippers pray in the Kushavatra tirtha *(ford or crossing) in Nasik during the Kumbha-mela festival. According to popular legend, the* kumbha *was a pot that held the nectar of immortality; when the gods tried to grab the pot, four drops of nectar splashed out and fell to earth. The four sites where the nectar fell are marked by the cities of Hardwar, Allahabad, Ujjain and Nasik, and the Kumbha-mela is held at each of these four holy sites in turn. Each event is attended by millions of pilgrims who travel to bathe in the sacred* tirthas *and to be blessed.*

The Hindu religious calendar overflows with feasts, festivals and fasts, commemorating everything from the births of deities and the passing away of spiritual teachers to unusual conjunctions of celestial phenomena and the sleep-cycle of Vishnu.

The greatest number of fasts, penitential rites and austerities are observed during the four months known as *caturmasa*. During this period (approximately mid-July to mid-November), which is also the rainy season, Vishnu naps: because the great preserver of the universe is unavailable, the weight of keeping order shifts to humans, and many devout Hindus are particularly careful about their diet and behaviour during this time. *Caturmasa* occurs during the sun's southern progression, when the days become shorter and darkness falls earlier, and special precautions are taken to guard against the evils associated with darkness. A two-week period (*pitr-paksha*) is set aside for pacifying the spirits of the deceased and honouring the ancestors. Like most rituals addressed to spirits and ancestors, these memorial rites (*shraddhas*) are observed in the "dark half", or waning fortnight, of the lunar month.

The key festivals observed during *caturmasa* celebrate the triumph of good over evil and darkness over light. The nine-night Navaratra honours the goddess Durga's vanquishing of the demon Mahisa (see p.43); Dasara is the culmination of the *Rama-Lila* festivities, which commemorate Rama's triumph over the evil Ravana (see p.22); and Tripura Purnima marks Shiva's conquest of the demons who, through various disguises and access to the nectar of immortality, were about to defeat the gods in battle. The Festival of Lights (Divali; see right) also occurs during *caturmasa*.

Many Hindu festivals, although now predominantly religious in their significance, were originally agricultural and seasonal events, and some still retain these connections. Pongal, which is widely celebrated in the south, comes after the first harvest and involves the ritual cooking and eating of the newly harvested rice. Holi marks the transition from winter to spring, cold to warmth, illness to health, and is popularly celebrated by throwing brightly coloured powders and eating sweets. On Naga-Pancami, farmers lay down their ploughs to recognize the snakes which may populate their fields, hoping by their appeasement to avoid snakebites; and on Pola, beasts of burden are given a day of rest and honoured with gifts of sweets and garlands.

In the Hindu religious calendar, feasts and fasts are assigned to particular lunar days, but there is great regional variation as to which festivals are celebrated and how these celebrations are conducted. Even religious New Year's festivals vary according to region and calendar, with some communities marking the New Year in the spring, others around October with Divali. Among the more popular festivals are the birthdays of Rama and Krishna; and Ganesha Cathurthi, which honours the elephant-headed deity Ganesha. Particular festivals are observed by women according to family custom,

including Vata-Savitri, which commemorates the epic princess Savitri's winning back her husband's life from the grip of Yama, the god of death.

A different type of festival is the *mela*, a huge fair that takes place at pilgrimage sites and usually lasts several days or weeks at particularly auspicious conjunctions of time. The best-known *mela* may be the Kumbha-mela (see left), celebrated about every three years in a twelve-year cycle and rotating among the cities of Hardwar, Ujjain, Nasik and Allahabad.

Feasts, fasts and holy days are part of the cadence of Hindu life and are designed to harmonize with the rhythm of the cosmos. By blessing life and celebrating sacred events and persons, they provide opportunities for the individual to share in sources of sanctity and auspiciousness.

DIVALI: THE FESTIVAL OF THE LIGHTS

The Festival of Lights, known as Divali or Dipavali, is one of the most widely observed festivals in India. It celebrates the triumph of light over darkness, fortune over misfortune and good over evil. On the moonless night that concludes the month of Ashvina (around October), Hindus invite Lakshmi, goddess of wealth and prosperity (see p.35), into their homes by lighting oil lamps which burn throughout the night, countering the threat of darkness, death and misfortune represented by Lakshmi's sister, Alakshmi.

The focal point of Divali is the worship of Lakshmi on the day of the new moon. Because for many communities this festival also marks the New Year, especially the new fiscal year, it is common to place before Lakshmi a sign of one's trade, with the hope that it will be blessed by the goddess, ensuring a prosperous year in business. The New Year is welcomed with gestures of prosperity: a luxurious oil bath, the wearing of new clothes, the exchange of sweets and the brilliance of fireworks in the night sky.

Young women light oil lamps during the Divali festival in New Delhi. The celebration continues for several days and includes the honouring of cows and their calves (symbols of fertility and prosperity); the presentation of gifts to family members; and the propitiation of restless spirits as well as of Yama, god of death.

SAINTS AND SAGES

In the Hindu religious tradition, individuals can be considered *tirthas* (centres of sacredness; see p.46): pilgrims approach living saints as well as the shrines of deceased saints to be in the presence of holiness and to receive blessings. The tradition of reverence for holy people dates at least from Vedic

A holy man meditates on passages from the Ramayana. *The marking on his forehead indicates that he is a worshipper of Vishnu.*

times, when the special sanctity of the *rishis* (sages or seers) who received and recited the wisdom of the Vedas was recognized. Today, such people are known as gurus or spiritual teachers, and are consulted on both spiritual and worldly matters. Many have large, international followings.

Some individuals are deemed saints by virtue of their accumulated spiritual knowledge; others because of their exemplary behaviour, their special abilities as spiritual teachers or their mystical experience of god. The Hindu tradition distinguishes between holy persons by using such appellations as *yogi* (practitioner of yoga), *guru* (personal spiritual guide), *sant* (devotional saint or mystic), *rishi* (sage or seer), *sadhu* (religious mendicant) and *swami* (spiritual teacher who is also an ascetic); but all can be considered saints because they live exemplary lives that are characterized by wisdom, devotion, discipline and service.

The life stories of many of the saints are well known, and some include manifestations of miraculous powers and episodes

Anandamayi Ma (1896–1982), a Bengali saint, is one of the most beloved of the contemporary Hindu gurus. She is considered an avatar of Mahadevi, the Great Goddess.

of intimate experiences of the divine. Some saints and teachers have also been social reformers, such as Vidyaranya (14th century), Ramadasa (19th century) Ramakrishna (19th century) and Gandhi (see right). Others, such as the Vaishnava saints Nammalvar and Andal, composed inspirational poetry and hymns that are still recited and sung. The great philosophers of India are also revered as teachers and holy men, in particular the influential Vedanta interpreters Shankara (8th century; see p.19), Ramanuja (died 1137; see p.19) and Madhava (13th century). In some sense all saints are teachers: by word or by example, they inspire other people to righteous living and the pursuit of truth, while giving them courage to face daily hardships.

In the *Upadeshasahasri*, a treatise on Vedanta philosophy, Shankara enumerates the qualities of a guru, among which is the sincere desire to help others. A guru is expected to be well versed in the sacred texts, possessed of self-control and compassion and free from all vices. The role of the spiritual teacher is emphasized throughout Hindu literature. In some schools of Hinduism, such as Tantra, the guidance of a guru is essential; in others, such as that of Shaiva Siddhanta, the guru is considered a manifestation of god. In many *bhakti* traditions (see p.31), devotees make no distinction between

MAHATMA GANDHI

Mohandas Karamchand Gandhi (1869–1948), known to the world as the Mahatma or "Great Soul", drew from the teachings of many religious traditions in his pursuit of truth, and his political activism took much of its inspiration from the teachings of Hinduism.

Greatly influenced by the *Bhagavad Gita* (see p.23), Gandhi believed in the importance of selfless action. He particularly advocated the practice of non-violence (*ahimsa*), one of the cardinal virtues of Hinduism. By his own example he demonstrated that non-violence was not a call to passivity, but a disciplined way of being actively and responsibly involved in this world. For Gandhi, *ahimsa* was not just a moral doctrine, but a social and political creed as well.

Gandhi's belief that the pursuit of truth is what leads to liberation (*moksha*) caused him to become actively involved in the political arena. In his autobiography he explains that his experience had taught him that "there is no other God than Truth". This religious realization drew him directly into politics: "those that say that religion has nothing to do with politics do not know what religion means."

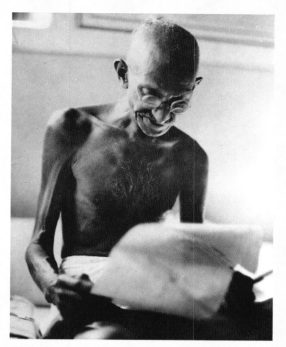

Mahatma Gandhi, photographed here in 1948, just before his assassination, helped to lead India toward independence and self-rule.

the goal (god) and the one who guides them toward that goal (the teacher). Many gurus trace their lineage to great gurus of the past, thereby establishing a claim to an unbroken, authoritative chain of teaching and knowledge.

In modern times, Hindus and non-Hindus in India and abroad have turned for guidance to Indian spiritual teachers. Ramakrishna (1836–86), a Bengali saint and mystic, taught that all religions are different paths to the same experience of god. His disciple, Swami Vivekananda, took this message to the World Parliament of Religions in Chicago in 1893, and since then their mystical teachings have found an intellectual as well as a spiritual home in the West.

Other gurus have had great emotional appeal, including Swami Narayana (1781–1830), leader of the Satsang sect; Sai Baba and his charismatic namesake Sathya Sai Baba (born 1926), considered avatars of Shiva; Ramana Maharishi (1879–1950), who taught using the question "Who are you?"; and Swami Shivananda (died 1964), a physician turned renunciant (*sannyasin*) who founded the Divine Life Society in Rishikesh. Devotees seek out such gurus to be in their presence and to receive their teachings and blessings: a touch or a glance from the teacher may impart his or her grace and love. However, as many great gurus are fond of reminding their students, the true teacher is to be found within oneself.

BUDDHISM

Some twenty-five centuries ago a great man took up the life of a wandering ascetic in what is today northern India. This in itself was not a unique event: many others also sought spiritual liberation walking in the forests. However, this man's quest resulted in answers that have been handed down to successive generations and, in the process, have been elaborated, interpreted and reinterpreted to form one of the greatest living religious traditions. In fact, Buddhism is much more than a religion: its cultural and philosophical impact has for centuries reverberated throughout south and Southeast Asia and, more recently, in the West. The tradition has become so vast and diverse that a superficial glance seems to reveal more disparity than continuity. Nevertheless, behind the many incongruities there is a recognizable common thread. All forms of Buddhism share the same roots, and all are motivated by the quest to attain a long-lasting state of contentment through mental, spiritual and moral development. All relate in some way to the enlightenment experience of one man, who is known as "the Buddha".

Buddhism began in India in the 5th century BCE and all its variants can be traced to these origins. The precise historical beginning of the tradition is somewhat obscure, although there is little reason to doubt that around the 5th century BCE an exceptionally charismatic teacher, probably a member of the

A giant statue in Leshan, Sichuan Province, China, preserves the image of Siddhartha Gautama, "the historical Buddha". The community of monks and nuns (Sangha) that the Buddha founded continues to transmit his teaching.

Shakya clan in Kapilavastu (in present-day Nepal), began to preach a new approach to the age-old problem of salvation. It has been suggested that his teaching was a reaction to the dominant *brahmanical* culture of his time, which centred on the Vedas (see pp.20–21) and on the sacrificial practices that were carried out by the priestly class. However, Buddhism exerted an enormous influence on the intellectual, religious and cultural life of India for more than sixteen centuries. It played a formative part in defining Hindu culture and, during its first centuries, was so enmeshed in Indian society (together with other spiritual teachings of the subcontinent) that it is misleading to think of it as a self-conscious reformist movement.

Buddhism became established as a monastic religion, enjoying spells of royal patronage, but around the 8th century CE it came under pressure from a resurgent Hinduism. Its decline was precipitated by Muslim invasions from the north, which began in the 7th century and gradually intensified during the following eight centuries. With the ruthless sacking of the great Buddhist universities at the end of the 12th century, Buddhism all but disappeared from India.

The teachings of Buddhism have never been exclusive to one class or limited to one geographical area. The Buddha and his monks spent the dry months wandering in what is today northern India and, long before Buddhism's disappearance from India, their beliefs were carried by monks and travellers all over Asia – to Sri Lanka, Burma, China, Thailand, Korea and Tibet, to name but a few of the places where the tradition has taken root. Buddhism is particularly amenable to expansion because of the universality of the Buddha's teaching. His *Dharma* (Truth) is designed to appeal to every individual, regardless of rank or class, inviting him or her to follow the path leading to enlightenment and the cessation of suffering. Being linked to neither a specific

KEY

Early Buddhism

Southern Buddhism

Northern Buddhism

Eastern Buddhism

● Modern cities

· Sacred sites

▲ Sacred mountains

Buddhism spread from India in all directions. The southern form has roughly 100 million adherents in Sri Lanka, Burma, Thailand, Cambodia and Laos. In the East (China, Korea and Japan) it is not possible to estimate numbers accurately, because of multi-religious practice and the suppression of religion by the Communists. In northern Buddhism, practised by Tibetans, Mongols, Bhutanese and Nepalese, numbers are again elusive, but estimates range between ten and twenty-five million.

place nor a single society, Buddhism has generally managed to incorporate the local customs and beliefs that it has encountered in its expansion, especially those that are traditionally associated with the social life. This has opened up Buddhism to a host of influences and has resulted in a greatly varied tradition, which nevertheless manages to preserve the core of its teaching.

AREAS OF MAJOR BUDDHIST ACTIVITY AND INFLUENCE IN ASIA

THE BUDDHA'S PREVIOUS LIVES
AND HIS FINAL BIRTH

For more than two millennia, the Buddha's life-story has been transmitted by generations of Buddhists, making it one of the most instructive explanations of the Buddhist path. Different renderings have emphasized different aspects of this great epic. For example, the Pali *Jatakanidana* (*c.*5th century CE) goes into great detail about the Buddha's previous lives, and the *Buddhacharita* (*c.*2nd century CE) begins with his last birth. The beautiful *Lalitavistara* emphasizes the supernatural, while many works of Western scholarship seek to uncover the facts behind the legend. All versions, however, share a common heritage, and it is the core of this legacy that is told here.

The *Jatakanidana* reports that many, many aeons ago, when another Buddha, Dipankara, was walking the earth, there lived a pure and virtuous man called Sumedha. He was born to a wealthy family but renounced his worldly possessions and became an ascetic. When Sumedha encountered Dipankara, he resolved that he too would become a Buddha, "one who has awakened" from the sleep of ignorance. This intention to attain enlightenment made him a *bodhisattva* (see pp.84–5). Dipankara saw that Sumedha would ultimately become fully enlightened, and subsequent Buddhas reaffirmed this prediction.

The *bodhisattva* was reborn many times and in many forms, perfecting himself in each life to become a Buddha. He sought to be more generous with fellow beings, to lead an impeccable moral life, to make do with as few possessions as possible, to cultivate his mental and psychic abilities, and to gain insight into the way things are. These and other perfections were later to become the hallmarks of his teaching and of Buddhism in general.

In his penultimate life the *bodhisattva* was reborn

At his final birth the buddha-to-be emerged from his mother's side, as shown in this Burmese laquerwork from the 1970s.

THE *JATAKA* STORIES

The *Jatakas* (Previous Birth Stories of the Buddha) are a collection of 547 edifying tales about the adventures of the Buddha in his previous lives. They share a common form, beginning by explicitly stating the moral of the story and ending by identifying who the Buddha (then only a *bodhisattva*) was in the tale. The Buddha appears in many guises, including those of a god, a trader, a bandit, a caravan leader, a deer, an antelope and a vulture.

These fables, some of which are based on pre-Buddhist folk tales, have been told time and time again. They have become completely ingrained in the lore of the many cultures to which Buddhism has spread and have inspired countless artistic representations. They are especially popular among the laity of Southeast Asian countries.

The *Jatakas* extol the virtues of leading a righteous life, which can help to ensure a favourable rebirth. For example, in the *Monkey-Lord Jataka*, the *bodhisattva* tricks a greedy crocodile by telling the predator that his monkey heart is hanging on a nearby tree, and thereby teaches the reptile the virtue of truth. In the famous *Vessantara Jataka*, where the *bodhisattva* appears as a prince, he teaches the merit of giving by parting with everything, including his children and wife.

The Jataka *stories about the Buddha's previous lives are popular to this day and have even been transformed into an Indian comic book series, as shown above.*

in the Tusita Heaven, where he prepared for his final birth among humans. From the Tusita Heaven he surveyed the world, choosing as his mother the virtuous Queen Maya, wife to Suddhodana, king of the Shakyas at Kapilavastu. The night on which the *bodhisattva* was conceived, the queen dreamed that an elephant touched her side and placed a white lotus in her womb, while at the moment of conception the 10,000 world systems quaked violently. The soothsayers who were summoned to explain the queen's dream said that she was pregnant and that the new child would be either a universal monarch or a Buddha, depending on whether he followed the life of a householder or that of an ascetic.

As the time of birth approached, the queen travelled toward Devadaha, where her parents lived, stopping to rest in the pleasure grove of the *sal* trees at the Lumbini gardens. Entering the gardens she felt the onset of labour, and a great *sal* tree bent gently to support her. The *bodhisattva* emerged from his mother's side – clean and pure, like a man descending a staircase – and was received into the golden net of the great gods (*brahma*s). Surveying the ten directions, he took seven strides to the north and roared: "I am the chief of the world. This is my last existence; henceforth there is no more rebirth for me." The miraculous birth was marked by great joy throughout the world: the blind could see, the crippled could walk and the deaf could hear the dumb. The world itself celebrated as the great ocean turned into sweet water and five kinds of lotuses covered the surface of the earth.

PRINCELY LIFE
AND THE GREAT RENUNCIATION

One of the most prominent features of the Buddha's life-story is the fact that in his final existence he was human. This information can be misleading, however, because he was much more than an ordinary person. Being a Buddha is being neither human nor god, but going beyond the nature of both. In spite of this distinction, the Buddhist tradition recalls the exemplary life of the

The indulgent splendour of princely life, depicted in a stone relief of the 2nd century CE.

Buddha in his human phase as a means of introducing the basic problem of human existence, the problem to which enlightenment is the solution.

After his final birth the *bodhisattva* was named Siddhartha, meaning "one whose goal is accomplishment". The seers immediately recognized that he was a special child. Even in infancy he bore the thirty-two marks of a great man, attesting to his uniqueness: these included his extended heels, long fingers, delicate skin, lion-like jaw and blue eyes. His mother, her mission accomplished, died seven days after his birth and was reborn amid the contented gods of the Tusita Heaven.

Siddhartha's future was prophesied twice and on both occasions it was revealed that he would be either a universal king, known throughout the lands for his power and justice, or a Buddha, leading a religious life and setting humankind free from ignorance. If Siddhartha followed the life of a householder he would become a great king, but if he renounced the world he would become a Buddha. King Suddhodana was told that in order to ensure

his son's royal future, he must prevent him from ever seeing the miseries of life. The king thus built three palaces for his son, and surrounded them with guards whose duty was to prevent the prince from seeing the true character of human experience.

Siddhartha Gautama was a unique and talented youth. His radiance knew no bounds and he excelled his contemporaries in skill and learning. Cushioned by all the imaginable delights of worldly life, he remained ignorant of the inevitable pain of the human condition. The *Buddhacharita* (see p.58) describes his splendid surroundings in great detail, evoking, for example, the soft voices and charming music of many dancing girls and the radiant pavilions suited to every season.

In time the prince married the fair Yasodhara, and at the age of twenty-nine it seemed as if he would proceed along the road to kingship without ever suspecting that outside the delights of his secure haven there was a much harsher reality. One day, however, he wished to see beyond the perimeter of his guarded dwellings. The king tried to dissuade him, but on failing in this attempt he ordered the city to be cleared of anything that might discomfort the prince. In four outings, known in the Buddhist tradition as "the Four Sights" (see right), Siddhartha encountered old age, disease, death and, finally, an ascetic who was seeking a way to transcend such suffering. He was deeply affected by this fourth encounter and vowed to abandon his princely life and seek the truth about the human condition.

Having taken this resolve, Siddhartha returned to the palace, where he was notified that his wife had given birth to a son. He could not find happiness in this, and retorted, "A fetter [*rahula*] has been born." The king consequently decreed that his grandson should be named Rahula. At the palace all attempts to entertain Siddhartha failed. He was no longer interested in the delights of the senses and merely fell asleep on the couch. When he awoke in the middle of

the night and saw the beautiful singers and dancers sprawled inelegantly over his parlour, they seemed to him like corpses and caused him mental anguish. He resolved to carry through his "great renunciation" that very night and instructed his charioteer Chandaka to prepare his great horse Kanthaka.

Before leaving the palace, he visited his wife's chambers. Standing at the threshold and smelling the jasmine, his heart was filled with longing. He saw the fair Yasodhara sleeping with her hand resting on

THE FOUR SIGHTS

Prince Siddhartha ventured beyond the palace walls four times, accompanied by his charioteer Chandaka, and the "Four Sights" that he encountered led to his renunciation of the world, one of the great turning points in his life.

On his first outing, Siddhartha saw a wasted man supporting himself with a stick. Chandaka explained that this was old age and that it was the fate of all living beings, including the prince. When

the king heard about the incident, he doubled the number of guards around his son and increased the number of his entertainers.

On his second outing, the prince came across a man afflicted with disease. Again Chandaka informed him that this misfortune can strike all living beings, including the prince. On his third outing, the prince saw a corpse, and Chandaka then discussed with him the nature and meaning of death.

At the palace Siddhartha became broody. No amount of entertainment could cheer him up: he was like "a lion pierced in the heart by a poisoned arrow". He could not understand how people could be at peace with themselves or indulge in laughter when old age, illness and death existed in the world. Years later he would teach that such suffering is always present, and would offer a solution to this predicament.

On his final outing, Siddhartha saw a monk carrying a begging bowl. Chandaka told him that this man had abandoned the household life and had "gone forth" to lead the holy life of an ascetic in search of truth and happiness. There and then Siddhartha resolved to do the same.

This detail from an 18th-century Burmese manuscript shows Prince Siddhartha encountering the Four Sights that would ultimately set him on the path to liberation.

Siddhartha's Great Departure is depicted in this 14th-century mural from the Wat Phra temple, Chiang Mai, Thailand.

Rahula, and felt the urge to pick his son up for the last time, but he did not dare to do so for fear that he might wake them and jeopardize his departure.

Under normal circumstances leaving the palace would have been impossible. There were hundreds of armed men at each of the town's massive gates. But one heavenly *deva* (god) gently swung open the gate while others muffled the sound of Kanthaka's hoofs and plunged the town's inhabitants into a deep slumber. Swiftly riding through the air, accompanied by celestial hosts of all kinds, Siddhartha, Chandaka and Kanthaka arrived at the river Anoma. There the *bodhisattva* bid Chandaka to return to the palace to inform his family of his departure. Kanthaka could not bear to part with his master and died on the spot.

He was reborn in the Tavatimsa Heaven, the heaven of the Thirty-three Gods.

Shedding his royal attire, the *bodhisattva* cut off his flowing hair with one stroke of his sword and tossed it into the air, saying, "If I am to become a Buddha, let it remain in the sky; if not, let it fall to the ground." With his divine eye, Indra, king of the gods, saw this gesture and caught the *bodhisattva*'s hair in a jewelled casket. The god Brahma offered the *bodhisattva* three saffron robes, an alms bowl and the other requisites of a monk: a razor, a needle, a water strainer and a belt. Siddhartha was now set on the irrevocable path to liberation, at the end of which he would attain perfect wisdom and completely extinguish the flame of suffering.

ENLIGHTENMENT: THE STRUGGLE
AND ITS REWARD

*A colossal Buddha in Pathein, Burma, sits in the earth-pointing position, which reflects the moment
of his enlightenment and final defeat of the demon Mara.*

As a prince, Siddhartha Gautama lived in unsur-passed luxury, but his great wealth could not lib-erate him from rebirth, old age, sickness and death. He thus relinquished all earthly pleasures and sev-ered his ties with society, setting out to wander through the forest to seek salvation. The practice of renunciation, modelled on the example of the Buddha, is still followed by Buddhist monks and nuns. The Buddha came to understand that renunci-ation in itself could not bring about the cessation of suffering. He acknowledged that much can be gained from leading the simple life of an ascetic, but also taught that extreme austerities are not conducive to the path of liberation.

In his search for enlightenment, the *bodhisattva* joined five ascetics who were practising the severest austerities in the hope of gaining ultimate insight.

In their company Gautama learned to endure the most extreme self-mortification, becoming weak and frail through starvation and pain. Even the magnifi-cent distinguishing marks that had adorned him since birth (the thirty-two marks of a great man; see p.60) almost disappeared. The *bodhisattva* who had known the greatest pleasure had now experienced its exact opposite.

Eventually he came to realize that nothing would be gained from extreme deprivation. As the god Indra demonstrated to him, if the strings of a lute are too tight they will break, and if they are too slack they will not play: only if they are properly strung will music issue forth. Gautama understood that the same balance is necessary with humankind and resolved to end the useless life of extreme asceticism by bathing and receiving food. Observing this change, his five companions deserted him, believing that he had admitted defeat and was therefore unworthy of them.

At the end of six years of varied experiences, Gautama decided to pave his own way: a middle path between the extremes of self-indulgence and self-mortification. On the banks of the river Nairanjana, he accepted an offering of rice-milk from a young girl named Sujata. He knew that enlightenment was near because the previous night he had had five premonitory dreams. He therefore divided Sujata's offering into forty-nine mouthfuls, one for each of the days he knew he would spend in contemplation following the night of his enlightenment.

"Roused like a lion", he proceeded to what would later become known as the Bodhi Tree, in Bodh Gaya (see p.65). After surveying the four cardinal directions, he sat in the lotus position underneath the tree and vowed not to move until he had attained complete and final enlightenment.

Rarely does a *bodhisattva* become a Buddha, and the onset of such an event sends ripples all throughout the world systems. Mara, the demon of all demons, sensed that Gautama was about to escape from his power and gathered his troops to oust the *bodhisattva* from his seat beneath the tree of enlightenment. The ensuing confrontation, in which Mara was soundly defeated, is one of the great stories of the Buddhist tradition.

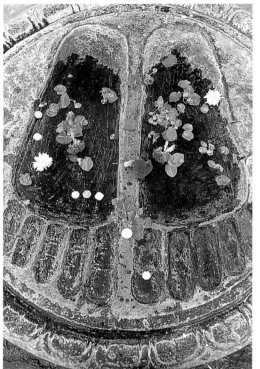

Offerings are left on a large stone representation of the Buddha's footprints adjacent to the Mahabodhi temple, Bodh Gaya. The prints are one of the most unequivocal signs of the Buddha's presence at this place of enlightenment.

Mara attacked the *bodhisattva* with nine elemental weapons, but to no avail: whirlwinds faded away, flying rocks and flaming spears turned into lotus flowers, clouds of sand, ashes and mud were transformed into fragrant sandalwood and, finally, the darkest of darknesses was outshone by the *bodhisattva*. Enraged, Mara turned to the buddha-to-be and demanded his seat. Gautama replied: "You have neither practised the ten perfections, nor renounced the world, nor sought true knowledge and insight. This seat is not meant for you. I alone have the right to it." Beside himself with rage, Mara flung his razor-edged disc at the buddha-to-be, but it turned into a garland of flowers above his head. Then Gautama challenged Mara: if the demon believed that he was entitled to occupy the seat of enlightenment, let him bring witnesses to his meritorious deeds. Mara turned to his fiendish companions, who submissively gave their testimony. He then asked the *bodhisattva* who would bear witness for him. Gautama drew out his right hand, pointed it downward and said, "Let this great solid earth be my witness." With this, a thunderous earthquake swept the universe and all the demons flew away. Even Mara's great elephant, Girimekhala, knelt down before the buddha-to-be.

After Mara's defeat, the gods gathered around Gautama while he set his mind on enlightenment. In India the night is divided into several "watches". In the first watch, the *bodhisattva* experienced the four successive stages of meditation, or mental absorptions (*dhyana*; see p.77). Freed from the shackles of conditioned thought, he could look upon his many previous existences, thereby gaining complete knowledge of himself.

In the second watch of the night, he turned his divine eye to the universe and saw the entire world as though it were reflected in a spotless mirror. He saw the endless lives of the many beings of the universe unfold according to the moral value of their deeds (karma; see pp.72–3). Some were fortunate, others miserable; some were beautiful, others ugly; but none ceased to turn in the endless cycle of birth and death (*samsara*; see p.72).

In the third watch of the night, Gautama turned his meditation to the real and essential nature of the world. He saw how everything rises and falls in tandem and how one thing always originates from another. Understanding this causal law of Dependent Origination (see p.74), he finally beheld the key to breaking the endless cycle of *samsara*, and with this understanding he reached perfection. It is said that he became tranquil like a fire when its flames have died down.

In the fourth and final watch of the night, as dawn broke, the *bodhisattva*'s great understanding enabled him to completely "blow out" (the literal meaning of nirvana) the fires of greed, hatred and delusion that had previously tied him to rebirth and suffering. At the moment of becoming a Buddha, his entire knowledge crystallized into the Four Noble Truths (*aryasatya*; see pp.74–5): the Noble Truth of *Duhkha* (suffering), the Noble Truth of the Origin of *Duhkha*, the Noble Truth of the Cessation of *Duhkha* and the Noble Truth of the Path Leading to the Cessation of *Duhkha*.

Although there are many accounts of the Buddha's night of enlightenment, at times varying in detail, there is complete unanimity about the Four Noble Truths. They can be said to contain the entire teaching of the Buddha, and consequently of Buddhism, and the extent to which they are understood is an indication of progress along the path: "to know" in Buddhism is to comprehend and realize the Four Noble Truths. Only a Buddha has complete and final understanding of their subtlest meaning, which is equal to enlightenment and nirvana.

BODH GAYA

It is common for pilgrims to visit the places connected with the Buddha's life and death, and Bodh Gaya, located in the Ganges basin (see map, p.57), is one of the holiest of Buddhist sites. It was here, on the night of the full moon of the month of Vesakha (May), that the *bodhisattva* sat under the Bodhi Tree, the "Tree of Enlightenment", and reached nirvana, releasing himself from the endless cycle of rebirth and becoming a Buddha. He remained under the Bodhi Tree for forty-nine days, meditating on the meaning of his awakening, before going out into the world to teach other beings about his discoveries. Bodh Gaya is said to be the only place on earth that can sustain the weight of the experience of enlightenment.

A pipal tree, descended from the Bodhi Tree under which the Buddha attained enlightenment, stands at Bodh Gaya, near to the Mahabodhi temple, built in the 6th century and subsequently restored.

THE BUDDHA'S TEACHINGS

The Buddha's enlightenment was in some respects the pinnacle of his achievement, but it was his subsequent teaching of *Dharma* (Truth) that laid the foundation for his enduring legacy. The community of monks and nuns that he established ensured the transmission of this doctrine to future generations, and in the 3rd century BCE the reign of the emperor Ashoka played an instrumental role in the dissemination of Buddhism in India (see below).

After he had attained nirvana, the Buddha remained for seven weeks at the site of the Bodhi Tree and enjoyed great bliss. During this period he realized that what he had come to understand was a profound and difficult truth, which other people, who relished worldly attachment, would find hard to grasp. He concluded that it would be pointless to try to teach others about his enlightenment, but the great god Brahma Sahampati intervened and

implored the Buddha to share his discoveries with humankind. Impelled by his great compassion, the Buddha decided to survey the world. He saw that beings are of different kinds: like lotuses in a pond, some are immersed underwater, others grow and rest on the surface, and others again come right out of the water and stand clear. He understood that just as some people have good qualities and others bad, some would be easy to teach and others would be difficult. Because of this diversity and out of his great compassion for all beings, the Buddha changed his mind and resolved to teach.

The Buddha's first sermon was addressed to the five ascetics who had been his companions before the enlightenment (see p.63). At the deer park at Sarnath (then called Isipatana), near present-day Varanasi (see map, p.57), he explained to them the content of his enlightenment in the form of the Four Noble

ASHOKA, A BUDDHIST EMPEROR

Buddhism began to flourish in the 3rd century BCE under the patronage of Emperor Ashoka, ruler of the Magadhan Empire which covered most of northern India. Ashoka abandoned a tradition of ruling by conquest and became engaged in setting up a kingdom governed according to Buddhist *Dharma*. Influenced by the teachings of the monastic community (Sangha), he expressed the desire to protect and please the people, and urged and rewarded

generosity. Ashoka inaugurated many public works to commemorate the Buddha and is largely responsible for the proliferation of stupas (relic mounds) and the cult of devotion at these stupas. His views and ordinances, through which he tried to implement Buddhist ideas, were recorded in his famous edicts carved on rocks and pillars throughout his empire.

This 3rd-century BCE Ashokan edict, on a pillar in Sarnath, promotes unity within the Buddhist faith.

Truths (see pp.74–5). The ascetics were so struck by the depth of his insight and the novelty of his message that one of them instantly became an *arhat*, a "worthy one" who attains nirvana through a Buddha's teaching (see pp.84–5). The other four followed suit in the days to come. This momentous first sermon, which has become one of the better-known articulations of the Buddha's teaching and of Buddhism in general, is called the "Setting in Motion of the Wheel of *Dharma*". It is still celebrated in most Theravada countries (see p.78) in the festival called Asalha Puja, which takes place on the full-moon day of the month of July.

For the next forty-five years, until his ultimate extinction, the Buddha taught *Dharma*. The number of his followers increased steadily and a community of monks, the Sangha (see pp.80–81), began to form. The Buddha himself continued wandering and begging for his food. He taught indiscriminately, talking to kings and paupers alike, and ceased travelling only in the three months of the rainy season.

The Buddha did not appoint a successor. When his disciples asked who would lead them after his death, he retorted that they must turn to themselves and be guided by the *Dharma* as he had taught it to them. It would be the duty of the Sangha to maintain the *Dharma* when he was gone.

As his death approached, the Buddha asked the assembled monks if they had any questions. The gathering remained silent. The Buddha's last words to the monks were, "All things composed are perishable. Now, strive diligently." Lying on his right side between two *sal* trees, he began meditating into the many stages of his complete and final extinction (*parinirvana*), after which he would never again be reborn. His body was cremated and, in accordance with his wish, the remains were divided among humans and gods. Stupas (dome-shaped funerary mounds) were erected over the relics. Stupas can be seen today at such sites as Sanchi and Amaravati in India, Anuradhapura in Sri Lanka and Borobudur in Indonesia (see map, p.57).

*At his final extinction (*parinirvana*), depicted by this giant 20th-century statue in Pegli, Burma, the Buddha reminded his followers that nothing is permanent, and instructed them to work toward the goal of liberation.*

THE BUDDHIST WORLD: "ALL IS *DUHKHA*"

The Buddha's teaching (*Dharma*), above all, offers a solution to the fundamental problem of the human condition. According to Buddhism, human existence is distinguished by the fact that nothing is permanent: no happiness will last forever, and whatever else there is, there will always be suffering and death. The first step in the Buddhist path to awakening is to recognize this as the foremost problem of human existence, to see that all is *duhkha*. However, this is not a pessimistic observation, because while acknowledging the ubiquity of *duhkha*, Buddhism offers a solution in the form of the Path Leading to the Cessation of *Duhkha* (see pp.76–7). The Buddha himself characterized his teaching by saying, "I teach only *duhkha* and the cessation of *duhkha*."

Duhkha can be experienced in three ways. The first is simply the "ordinary" suffering that affects people when the body is in pain. Ordinary suffering is also mental pain: it is the grief of not getting what one wants or the distress caused by separation from loved ones or from pleasant conditions. It is also the many other painful situations that one inevitably encounters by virtue of being born, ageing and dying. Underlying any happiness is the knowledge that whenever there is pleasure or delight, it will not be permanent. Sooner or later the vicissitudes of life will bring about a change. There is a Buddhist saying that even in laughter there is *duhkha*, because all

MANDALAS

Mandalas are both symbolic representations of the Buddhist world and meditational aids – testimony to the fact that there is no clear divide in Buddhism between cosmology and psychology. As cosmograms they are maps of the universe, while as meditational aids they are psychological tools, which assist the meditator to experience different states of mind. By concentrating on a *mandala* ("circle" in Sanskrit) the individual can progress toward an understanding of the reality of the world as perceived by Buddhism.

Mandalas, which take various forms, are often two- and three-dimensional. They range from temporary images in sand to paintings and vast stone structures. Simple coloured discs (*kasinas*) can also serve as meditational aids.

The 9th-century Buddhist monument of Borobudur in Indonesia takes the form of a mandala. *Its many terraces contain stone reliefs depicting the Buddha's life-story.*

laughter is impermanent. This instability underlies the second kind of *duhkha*, which is the dissatisfaction arising from change.

It might seem that only death can bring about the cessation of *duhkha*, but in fact death is also a form of *duhkha*. In Buddhism the cosmos extends far beyond the immediate physical world perceptible by the senses, and death is merely part of the endless cycle of rebirth, *samsara* (see p.72). Death in itself offers no respite because actions have consequences in future lives, far beyond death – just as deeds from previous lives have affected the present.

The third kind of *duhkha* is the inherent interconnectedness of actions and deeds, which exceeds human vision and experience. In this sense, *duhkha* applies to the universe in its totality, and no imaginable beings – humans, gods, demons, animals or hell beings – are exempt from it. *Duhkha* thus refers not only to everyday suffering but also to the whole infinite world of possible and seemingly endless forms of suffering. No simple translation can capture its full significance.

The goal of Buddhism is the complete and final cessation of every form of *duhkha*, and thereby the attainment of nirvana – the eradication of greed, hatred and delusion, which tie beings to the cycle of rebirth. Accordingly, Buddhas and those who reach enlightenment do not experience *duhkha*, because strictly speaking they are not "beings", nor do they "roll" in *samsara*: they will never again be reborn.

Duhkha characterizes the cosmos as a whole, but its predominance varies among the different "spheres of existence" (see p.72). In the World of Pure Form, where the great gods dwell, there is less suffering than in the World of Sense-Desire, inhabited by lesser gods, humans and other beings. Just as the Buddha when he walked the earth could enter the World of the Sense-Desire, so too can humans enter the World of Pure Form. This is ordinarily accomplished in meditation, through different kinds

The stones of the 13th-century Buddhist temple complex at Angkor, Cambodia, disintegrate beneath the clinging roots of a giant fig tree. According to the Buddha, all conditioned existence is impermanent, subject to decay and marked by a suffering rooted in the grips of craving, which can be overcome by following the path to enlightenment.

of absorptions (*dhyana*; see p.77). The characteristic form of suffering in this situation is impermanence, caused by the meditator's inability to remain eternally in trance. To attain more abiding happiness, an individual must strive to understand the processes that govern movement in the cosmos as a whole – namely, rebirth and karma (see pp.72–3) – and how they can be affected.

OVERLEAF *A statue of the Buddha stands on the crest of a hill at the Po Lin monastery, Hong Kong. Buddhism spread to China in the 2nd century* CE *and coexisted for centuries with both Confucianism and Daoism.*

REBIRTH AND KARMA

The idea of rebirth is not unique to Buddhism (see p.26), but it plays an important role in both its doctrine and its practice. The Buddha himself is said to have attained nirvana after a long series of rebirths, and on the night of his enlightenment, according to the Pali Canon, he remembered more than 100,000 previous lives.

All beings are continuously reborn in a seemingly endless cycle of birth and death (*samsara*). Just as a person's birth is not the beginning of his or her fortunes, so death is not the end, because all beings "wander" through successive incarnations: gods can become humans, humans can become gods, animals or hell beings, animals can become humans or "hungry" ghosts, and so on. Advanced beings, such as *bodhisattvas* (see pp.84–5), are able to avoid disadvantageous rebirths, but only Buddhas and *arhats* (see p.84) are fully liberated from *samsara*, because after their last lives they will never again be reborn.

The countless sentient beings who pass through *samsara* are accommodated in successive world systems, "as numerous as there are sands on the banks of the Ganges". Each world system is divided into three "spheres of existence". The crudest of these spheres is the World of Sense-Desire, governed by the five senses and inhabited by lesser gods (*devas*), humans, animals and the various hell beings. More refined is the World of Pure Form, where the greater gods dwell. This sphere corresponds to the four meditational absorptions (*dhyanas*; see p.77) and its beings are without the senses of touch, taste and smell. The most refined *samsaric* sphere of existence is the Formless World, a purely mental realm, devoid of the physical. Accomplished great gods are born here, but even these rebirths end, because although these gods have reached "summits of existence", they have not attained nirvana. Each of the world systems

lasts incalculable aeons: the *Samyutta Nikaya* of the Pali Canon, part of the Buddha's discourses (see p.82), explains that if a mountain of granite, seven miles (11.25km) high, were stroked every century with a piece of silk, it would be worn away before such a great aeon would pass.

Not every form of Buddhism subscribes to this exact cosmology, but all agree that rebirth is not a haphazard process. Just as a physical object is governed by a causal physical law, so a person's "spiritual" development is governed by a "natural" law, karma, which is inherent in the cosmos. According to the law of karma, every action or deed "ripens" as a certain kind of result. This law in itself is neither

A monk gazes into the distance from the colonnade of a monastery in Rangoon, Burma. The Buddha's teaching offers a way to break the bonds of samsara, *the succession of birth and rebirth that characterizes all existence.*

Milindapanha (*c.*1st–2nd century CE), a dialogue between the monk Nagasena and the king Milinda, Nagasena explains that deeds are linked to their outcomes in the same way that a mango tree's seed is linked to its fruit. A man who steals from another man's tree deserves a beating, even though he did not take the seed of the tree, because the stolen fruit could not have grown if the seed had not been planted.

The outcome of karma can be affected by good or bad deeds, which bring about favourable or unfavourable results. This gives rise to the psychological and ethical dimensions of karma. Every intentional deed is accompanied by a different kind of state of mind. If these states of mind are rooted in empathy, wisdom and lack of greed, then they are considered morally wholesome – and are karmically profitable. If, however, a deed is accompanied by states of mind rooted in hatred, delusion or greed, then it is morally unwholesome, and can lead to bad karma. For example, although generosity is a morally wholesome deed, it is the attitude behind the deed, be it mere friendliness or deep compassion, that determines the "karmic seed" which will generate the deed's "fruit". Ultimately, the goal of Buddhism is to teach sentient beings gradually to extinguish the fires of hatred, delusion and greed, thereby ceasing to generate bad karmic seeds, and finally, in realizing nirvana, to blow them out completely (nirvana literally meaning "blow out").

Karma underscores the importance of human life, because most good or bad deeds are performed in the human realm. Gods enjoy the fruits of their previous good deeds, while those reborn in the sub-human realms have little scope for making virtuous or non-virtuous deeds. As karma runs its course, these less fortunate beings may eventually obtain a more advantageous rebirth.

moral nor retributive but merely a feature of the constituent elements of *samsara*. Without karma any talk of enlightenment would be senseless: one could not strive toward enlightenment if there were no way to affect one's development.

Karma operates on intentional deeds and creates residual impressions or tendencies that bear fruit or "ripen" with time. Its effects are not limited to the present life but unfold over longer periods by creating favourable or unfavourable rebirths. In the

THE FOUR NOBLE TRUTHS

In a famous passage in the *Majjhima Nikaya* of the Pali Canon, the Buddha likens his teaching to a raft. Suppose, he says, a traveller sees a great expanse of water. The shore he stands on is dangerous and frightening, while the opposite shore offers safety, peace and tranquillity. There is neither a bridge to cross nor a ferry to carry him over, so he builds a raft. Once on the other shore, what should he do? Drag the raft that had been useful to him and turn it into an impediment, or let go of it now that he is safely across the water? The raft, the Buddha observes, is for crossing with, not clinging to, and the same is true of his teaching. It is neither an intellectual endeavour nor a creed, but merely something to be brought into being and cultivated.

The Buddha's teaching is most succinctly expressed in the Four Noble Truths (*aryasatya*), one of the most universally accepted formulations of Buddhism. These Truths proclaim *duhkha* and its cessation, and reflect the content of the Buddha's enlightenment. According to tradition, he expounded them in his first sermon delivered to his five former companions at the deer park near Sarnath (see pp.66–7). This sermon is called the "Setting in Motion of the Wheel of *Dharma*", and constitutes one of the most basic teachings of Buddhism.

The first Noble Truth is the Truth of *Duhkha*. The Buddha said that everything is *duhkha*: birth, ageing, sickness, death, parting, unfulfilled desires, decay, the state of all phenomena constantly changing – any experience, whether pleasurable or painful, is *duhkha*. *Duhkha* is the condition of universal impermanence which affects everything. Even the "I" or "Self" has no enduring quality, because in reality it is merely an error arising from false conceptualization. This doctrine of "no-self" (*anatman*) is one of the three characteristics of all conditioned existence, together with *duhkha* and impermanence.

The second Noble Truth, the Truth of the Origin of *Duhkha*, explains that *duhkha* arises from craving (literally, "thirst": *trishna*): craving for sensual pleasure, for having more or for having less, for existence and for self-annihilation. Such craving or greed is part of a cycle that is described as the twelve-linked chain of Dependent Origination (*pratityasamutpada*): it arises from feeling, which in turn arises from sense-contact, which arises from the six senses, which arise from mind and form, which arise from consciousness, which arises from formations, which arise from ignorance, which arises from suffering, which arises from birth, which arises from becoming, which arises from grasping, which arises from craving, and thus round and round again. One of the most celebrated principles of Buddhism, Dependent Origination underlies karma, causality, change and free will, and the way in which all conditioned phenomena exist. It is usually described as beginning with ignorance or confusion (*avidya*).

The third Truth is the Noble Truth of the Cessation of *Duhkha*. This truth asserts that there is an end to *duhkha*: supreme and final liberation is the "blowing out" of the fires of greed, hatred and delusion, that occurs when the cause of *duhkha* is removed. When Dependent Origination is fully understood and its consequences drawn out, when the chain is broken and the craving that leads to endless births and deaths is abandoned, complete and final cessation of *duhkha* is achieved. The Buddha calls the third Noble Truth "the Cessation" (*nirodha*). This is not identical to nirvana. Nirvana is not an effect produced by a cause: if it were, it would arise dependently, and if it arose dependently, it would not be able to offer a means of escape from the clutches of karma and rebirth.

Craving, which the second Noble Truth identifies as the origin of duhkha, *is part of the twelve-linked chain of Dependent Origination. Beginning with ignorance and culminating with the whole mass of suffering, this chain represents the grip of* samsara. *In this 20th-century Tibetan* thang ka *(painting on cloth), the chain of Dependent Origination is depicted on a wheel that is held in the clutches of the demon Mara. Such "wheels of becoming" are usually positioned at the entrances to monasteries in Tibet.*

The fourth Truth, the Noble Truth of the Eightfold Path, identifies the factors leading to the cessation of *duhkha*: right speech, right action, right livelihood, right effort, right mindfulness, right concentration, right view and right thought. These eight factors affirm the three essential elements of Buddhist spiritual training – moral conduct, concentration and wisdom (see pp.76–7).

The Four Noble Truths are commonly explained by use of a medical allegory. In the First Noble Truth the human condition is diagnosed as being *duhkha*. The Second Noble Truth cites craving as the cause of this malady. The Third Noble Truth makes a prognosis about the condition, proclaiming that recovery is possible. Finally, the Fourth Noble Truth, the Eightfold Path to the Cessation of *Duhkha*, is the medicine prescribed to restore the patient's health.

It is also customary to associate some sort of activity with each of the four Truths. The first Truth is to be "fully comprehended". The second needs to be eradicated: it requires thirst to be quenched. The third Truth is to be realized, to be made into reality. And the fourth is to be cultivated, "to be brought into being" – that is, to be kept and followed. The entire Buddhist *Dharma* can be seen as an elaboration of the Four Noble Truths.

THE PATH LEADING TO
THE CESSATION OF *DUHKHA*

Much description and elaboration of the Buddhist Path has been preserved in canonical texts and commentaries, such as the 5th-century BCE Maunggun gold plates, shown here, which are among the earliest Buddhist texts to be discovered in Burma.

A monk named Malunkyaputta once asked the Buddha complicated questions about the nature of the universe and the soul and fate of a Buddha after death. The Buddha told him that, by asking these questions, he was acting like a man wounded by an arrow who refused to be treated until he learned who had shot him, what his class was, where he came from and what kind of arrow he had used. Surely the man would die before these issues were resolved. A fundamentally practical teaching, the Buddha's way avoids speculation and focuses only on questions that are conducive to the holy life and to the cessation of *duhkha*: all else is immaterial to the Path.

The Eightfold Path to the Cessation of *Duhkha*, enumerated in the fourth Noble Truth (see pp.74–5), is the Buddha's prescription for the suffering experienced by all beings. It is commonly broken down into three components: *shila* (morality), *samadhi* (concentration) and *prajna* (wisdom). Another approach identifies a path beginning with *dana*, the virtue of giving. *Dana* underlies *shila*, which in turn enables a person to venture into higher aspirations. *Shila*, *samadhi* and *prajna* are at the core of Buddhist spiritual training and are inseparably linked. They are not merely appendages to each other like petals of a flower, but are intertwined like "salt in the great ocean", to invoke a famous Buddhist simile.

Shila (morality), described in the Eightfold Path as "right speech, right action and right livelihood", involves such customary moral imperatives as abstaining from telling lies and from killing. In everyday Buddhist practice *shila* follows from giving (*dana*), which is considered the primary ethical activity. *Dana* is more than just charity or generosity, because it has a strict religious meaning. Its focus is the community of monks (Sangha; see pp.80–81), and it is a great virtue for laypeople to offer the monks such everyday essentials as food, lodging, clothing and medicine. The members of the Sangha practise *dana* too, by sharing the greatest gift of all: the teaching of *Dharma*.

Shila is cultivated by following either five or ten precepts, or "rules of training". Both laity and Sangha undertake the so-called "Five Precepts", which underlie all Buddhist ethics: (i) to abstain from taking or destroying life; (ii) to abstain from taking what is not given; (iii) to abstain from misconduct with regard to sensual pleasure (sexual misconduct); (iv) to abstain from false speech and (v) to abstain from intoxicants (such as drugs and alcohol) that cloud the mind. Monks and nuns follow five additional precepts (see p.81). These rules of training are not only observed in practice but also taken as vows in the form of ritual chanting.

The second part of the Eightfold Path, the perfection of *samadhi* (concentration), involves "right effort, right mindfulness and right concentration". Cultivated in yoga and meditation, *samadhi* is neither an alternative to morality nor an optional extra. Like other Indian religions, Buddhism views the mind as the prime vehicle of salvation and emphasizes its proper training. Right effort is geared toward producing wholesome states of mind and preventing unwholesome states of mind; while right mindfulness develops awareness of feelings, bodily activities and mental activities. This training leads to right concentration, which is the attainment, in meditation, of various ecstatic altered states of consciousness (*dhyana*), enabling the experience of great joy.

The last part of the Path, "right view and right thought", constitutes *prajna* (wisdom). To attain *prajna*, to penetrate the reality of things directly, is tantamount to liberation in Buddhism. *Prajna* must be preceded by both *shila* and *samadhi* and is usually developed from the uniquely Buddhist practice of insight meditation (see below). The quest for *prajna* may also involve a conceptual or philosophical investigation of *Dharma* and of how the world is experienced. In their more technical senses, right view is the understanding of the Four Noble Truths and right thought is the loving kindness and compassion that free the mind from lust, ill-will and cruelty.

CALM MEDITATION AND INSIGHT MEDITATION

Buddhist meditation (*bhavana*) is based on two methods – *shamatha* (calm) and *vipashyana* (insight) – both of which are necessary vehicles on the Eightfold Path to the Cessation of *Duhkha*.

Shamatha meditation aims at achieving calmness and concentration, and at raising the perception of the meditational subject to the point of abstraction. After mental obstacles have been eliminated, the mind "absorbs" itself into an abstract idea of the subject: this absorption is called *dhyana* (in Pali, *jhana*; in Chinese, *ch'an*; in Japanese, *zen*). Different meditational "aids" give rise to different mental absorptions. A beginner might concentrate on a coloured disc (*kasina*), while a more advanced practitioner could focus on recollecting the Buddha.

The goal of *vipashyana* meditation is to realize wisdom (*prajna*). This is also acquired gradually and ultimately achieved through the mental absorptions of *shamatha* meditation. The practitioner aims to directly comprehend the three characteristics of the phenomenal world: impermanence (*anitya*), *duhkha* and "no-self" (*anatman*).

A novice monk in serene meditation at the Zen monastery of Eihei-ji, Japan.

DIFFERENT VISIONS OF THE PATH

The Buddha did not appoint a successor, and after his final extinction Buddhism never again had a central authority. With the passage of time and the tradition's geographical expansion, it was inevitable that different visions of the Buddhist path developed. However, such divergences have never constituted a schism, because varying views are, and always have been, permissible in Buddhism. Only by changing the rules of monastic practice, and thereby splitting the Sangha, would a schism be created.

There are different visions of the Buddhist Path, but serenity is a common theme in Buddhist doctrine, as reflected in this giant Buddha statue in Chiang Rai, Thailand.

In the Pali *Nikayas* it is said that before his final extinction the Buddha urged his followers to make themselves and the *Dharma* their only "island" and sole refuge. Accordingly, after his death the members of the Sangha gathered in Rajagriha (present-day Rajgir; see map, p.57) to recite the Buddha's discourses. This event is referred to as the First Council. As the Sangha spread and Buddhist thought developed, it was inevitable that disputes would arise. By the time the Second Council was called at Vesali (*c.*330BCE), there were many factions in the Sangha pulling in different directions.

The more conservative form of Buddhism, the Theravada (Teaching of the Elders), is the dominant form practised today in such places as Sri Lanka (see right), Burma and Thailand. Theravadins emphasize the importance of the last, "historical" Buddha – Siddhartha Gautama – and claim to preserve his authentic teaching. This teaching is canonized as the "Three Baskets" (*Tipitaka*; see p.82), a group of texts dating probably from the 1st century BCE and written in Pali, a middle Indian language akin to the language the Buddha himself would have spoken. Classical Theravada recognizes that there are different goals for different followers. However, its ideal is the *arhat* (see p.84), the disciple who gains enlightenment through meditation on the Buddha's *Dharma*, and is released from the cycle of rebirth.

An alternative understanding of the Buddhist goal began to emerge around the time of the Second Council, although its exact origins are not clear. This strand of Buddhism was later called Mahayana, or "Greater Vehicle", and today it is the dominant form of Buddhism in China, Japan and Tibet. Unlike Theravada Buddhism, which is still a relatively unified tradition, the Mahayana constitutes a variety of different schools, such as the Japanese Tendai and Pure Land (see p.87). However, the Mahayana never formed its own monastic code. Mahayana monks can practise alongside monks of other traditions, even though they may have different aspirations or visions of the Path.

The Mahayana accepts Gautama as a Buddha but greatly expands the notion of Buddhahood by recognizing a rich "pantheon" of Buddhas and *bodhisattvas* ("those whose essence is enlightenment"; see pp.84–5). It also produced scriptures that are not accepted by other forms of Buddhism as the word

BUDDHISM IN SRI LANKA

According to legend, Buddhism was established in Sri Lanka in the 3rd century BCE by the monk Mahinda, son of Ashoka (see p.66). Sinhalese Buddhism is certainly an ancient tradition, and many of the great commentaries of the Pali Canon (see p.82) – for example, Buddhaghosa's *Vissuddhimaga* – originate from the island. Sri Lanka became a predominantly Theravadin kingdom, with a strong Sangha and rulers who promoted the Buddhist Truth (*Dharma*). The close link between the populace and the Sangha, produced by the monastic community's reliance on the laity and royal patronage, has made the island a distinctively Buddhist country and coloured its culture and heritage.

The history of Buddhism in Sri Lanka reflects the island's tumultuous past. In 1815, when the British took over the island (then called Ceylon), they opened the doors to Christian missionaries. Sinhalese Buddhism, responded by becoming more "rational" and less "religious", and also by reasserting itself as a living force in society. With national independence in 1947, the Sangha assumed new social and political responsibilities, in particular becoming closely connected with the country's education system.

Buddhist temples, such as the Weherahena temple, shown here, can be found all over Sri Lanka.

of the Buddha (see pp.82–3). Broadly speaking, the Mahayana differs from the Theravada in its representation of the final goal that a Buddhist follower should seek. Expanding the Theravadin ideal of the *arhat*, who devotes himself to gaining insight, it offers the path of the *bodhisattva* as the ultimate accomplishment. Through the perfection of wisdom and compassion, the *bodhisattva* teaches others so that they too may achieve enlightenment. The Mahayana considers other paths as inferior to that of the *bodhisattva*, referring to them derogatively as "Hinayana" (Lesser Vehicle).

A characteristic feature of Mahayana Buddhism is the notion that Buddhas or advanced *bodhisattvas* can, through their immense powers, create "Buddha Fields" or "Pure Lands". These Pure Lands are seen as unique and blissful paradises, which are accessed by a favourable rebirth following a life of devotion to the presiding Buddha. In a Pure Land a being is able to hear and practise *Dharma* in conducive circumstances, enabling swift enlightenment. Of the many Pure Lands, the Pure Land of the West, ruled by the Buddha Amida (in Sanskrit, Amitabha), is one of the most important (see p.86).

THE BUDDHIST COMMUNITY

Young Burmese monks make their daily alms round. "Taking the robe" for three months initiates them into adulthood.

Traditionally, to be a Buddhist means to take refuge in the "three jewels" (*triratna*): the Buddha, the *Dharma* and the Sangha. The Sangha in this context is the noble community (*ariya-sangha*) of Buddhist saints who have realized the teaching. The word also designates the community of monks and nuns who live according to the monastic code (*vinaya*); and in its broadest sense it includes the laypeople who sustain the monks and nuns through charity and receive their teaching.

The creation of the Sangha is without question one of the Buddha's most remarkable achievements. It has survived through diversification and expansion up to the present day, offering an individual the chance to pursue the course of training leading to enlightenment, by dedicating him or herself to the holy life. Such a pursuit would not be deemed a selfish act in Buddhist eyes, because the Sangha, as an institution, maintains the *Dharma* in the absence of the Buddha for the welfare of all.

From its earliest days the Sangha has lacked a supreme authority, because the Buddha refused to establish a functional hierarchy or name a successor. Influence is collective and precedence is allowed only by seniority. According to the Buddha, adherence to the *Dharma* should be based on personal reasoning and experience, not purely on instruction. A novice receives the teaching from an accomplished instructor, who in turn has been trained by another master, and thus, in theory at least, the chain extends to the Buddha himself. The idea of a lineage is central to the Sangha: the dominance of the master–pupil relationship compensates for the absence of a central power by shifting the burden of authority to the personal level.

In the beginning a follower was accepted into the Sangha with the simple words *ehi bhikku* ("Come, O monk"), but as numbers grew and the community dispersed, regulations were established. Every Buddhist undertakes the "Five Precepts" in the cultivation of the moral life (*shila*; see p.76), and monks and nuns follow five additional precepts, which are elaborated as training rules and referred to collectively as the *pratimoksha*. The five additional precepts are to abstain from eating after midday, from dancing and singing, from personal adornments, from using high seats or beds, and from handling gold or silver. The number of rules in the *pratimoksha* varies among the different traditions, although there is a common core of approximately 150. In the Theravadin tradition, there are 227 rules for monks and 311 for nuns. Every fortnight these rules are recited communally, providing an occasion for the members of the Sangha to confess any breaches.

Monks give up all worldly belongings and possess only a bare minimum of personal goods (an alms bowl, three robes, a belt, a razor and a needle). Traditionally they live as wandering religious beggars, settling in one place only for the three months of the rainy season. The monks rely on the charity of the laity for food and other subsistence, such as clothing, shelter and medicine. Expulsion is rare and enforced only in extreme cases, although a monk or nun may always leave the Sangha if he or she wishes.

The Sangha plays an extremely important role in Buddhism as the protector and maintainer of the *Dharma*. As early as the 1st century BCE, the Theravadin Sangha distinguished between monks who assumed the duty of meditating and those who were committed to preserving the scriptures. The core of "institutional" Buddhism, at least in the Theravadin tradition, has almost always been preoccupied with preserving the *Dharma* through the lineage of a committed community rather than through political power structures. This is one of the essential features that distinguishes Buddhism from religions that actively participate in – and indeed, govern – the passage of life through rites and rituals. It is not the norm for Buddhism to be linked to a specific place or society, which is why it has generally been able to coexist harmoniously with the indigenous beliefs and practices it has encountered in its expansion, especially those that are traditionally associated with social customs. In Japan, for example, it is said that a person is born Shinto and dies Buddhist, a distinction that affirms the salvation aspect of the Buddha's teaching (see pp.160–61).

The relationship between the Sangha and the laity varies greatly among the different traditions. Theravadin monks do not handle money or make a living from any profession, but rather rely completely on the laity for worldly needs. In such places as China and Japan, on the other hand, where Mahayana Buddhism is dominant, some monasteries have been known to accumulate great wealth and political power.

CANONS AND *SUTRAS*

A 12th-century CE manuscript of the Perfection of Wisdom Sutra *shows the* bodhisattvas *Avalokiteshvara (top) and Maitreya (bottom). Such sacred texts were written on palm leaves and then threaded together (the word "sutra" literally means "thread").*

After the Buddha's death the task of preserving his teachings began. His disciples met at the First Council in Rajagriha (present-day Rajgir; see map, p.57) to create an established version of the discourses on *Dharma* and *vinaya* (the rules of monastic conduct; see pp.80–81). As would have been common at the time, this record was not written down but was committed to memory and transmitted orally. To safeguard the integrity of the doctrine, formulaic expressions, repetitions, numerical lists and other mnemonic devices were incorporated. In addition, different monks specialized in memorizing particular sections of the teaching.

The Pali Canon, preserved by Theravada Buddhism, is the only complete text that has survived in an ancient Indian language. Produced in Sri Lanka around the 1st century BCE, it was written in Pali, a middle Indo-Aryan dialect akin to Magadhi, the language that was probably spoken by Gautama. The Canon is composed of the "Three Baskets" (*Tipitaka*), which are all considered to be "the word of the Buddha". The *Tipitaka* comprises some twenty-nine separate works, organized according to subject matter: the collection on monastic discipline (*Vinaya-pitaka*); the discourses of the Buddha (*Sutta-pitaka*), which includes the "Five Collections" (*Nikayas*); and the further teachings (*Abhidamma-pitaka*). The *Tipitaka* and its commentaries are the primary texts of Theravada Buddhism, and Pali has become the common language of Buddhist Southeast Asian culture, akin to Latin in medieval Europe. Other ancient records of these teachings survive in translation, most notably as parts of Chinese and Tibetan canons.

The *suttas* (in Sanskrit, *sutras*) of the Pali Canon are believed to be the word of the Buddha, but around the 2nd century BCE another genre of Buddhist scriptures began to emerge, which also claimed to quote the Buddha directly. It probably originated in the visionary experiences of certain monks and unquestionably represented a minority and non-conformist trend. So precious were these new *sutras* in the face of the overwhelming status of the canonized works that, untypically, they were set down in writing. The written *sutras* were revered, and many were said to have been hidden by the Buddha until the right time arrived for their dissemination. Written in a mixture of middle Indo-Aryan dialect and Sanskrit, they are referred to collectively as the "Mahayana *sutras*".

In time, and especially with the expansion of Buddhism toward north and northeast Asia (China, Korea, Japan and Tibet), these *sutras* gained importance and became the foundation of entirely new teachings, some of which were based on one particular *sutra* or on a collection of *sutras*. Approximately 600 survive today, despite the fact that they were never systematically organized into a coherent body. Among the many important Mahayana *sutras* are those that gave rise to schools or sects. For example, the *Perfection of Wisdom sutras* are associated with the rise of the Madhyamaka school of philosophy (see p.85); the *Lotus Sutra* had its own following (see below); the composite *Avatamsaka Sutra* was crucial to the foundation of Hua-yen Buddhism in China; and the assorted *Sukhavati sutras* were instrumental to the development of Japanese Pure Land Buddhism (see p. 87).

In addition to *sutra* material, Buddhism has a vast number of commentaries and polemical treatises that are attributed not to the Buddha but to inspired poets and scholarly teachers. These texts (*shastras*) exist in every form of Buddhism and are as much part of the Buddhist tradition as the *sutras*. They include textual exegeses, psychological elaborations, philosophical speculations, literature and poetry, and are written mostly in Pali, Sanskrit, Chinese, Japanese and Tibetan.

THE *LOTUS SUTRA*

The *Lotus Sutra* ("The Sutra on the Lotus of the Good *Dharma*") is one of the most popular and influential discourses of Mahayana Buddhism, especially in China and Japan. Extant in Sanskrit, its oldest parts probably date from the 1st century BCE or later. It is a beautiful and lucid text, set in verse and elaborated in prose (it is generally assumed that the verse pre-dates the prose).

The *Lotus Sutra* is delivered by the Buddha at Vulture Peak Rock, near Rajagriha (present-day Rajgir), in front of a great assembly of disciples and teachers. Using various parables he explains that there is only one vehicle to salvation, emphasizing the importance of the skilful use of means (*upaya*) in teaching and perfecting wisdom. The role of morality, emptiness and compassion is stressed in the path of the *bodhisattva*.

The *sutra* supposedly has magical powers in its own right, and great merit accrues for those who extol and disseminate it.

An illustration from a 17th-century Japanese version of the Lotus Sutra *shows the Buddha teaching the* Dharma. *The image is from a set of scrolls that was dedicated to the first Tokugawa shogun, Ieyasu (see p.150), and is kept in his mausoleum in Nikko, Japan.*

ARHATS, BODHISATTVAS AND OTHER GREAT TEACHERS

In addition to Gautama and other Buddhas, Buddhism recognizes a great many advanced beings. Some of these are human, some merely manifest themselves as human, and others exist only in trance and visualization. Most teach the *Dharma*, but others receive it. Some are shared by the majority of Buddhist traditions, while others are revered only by certain schools.

Buddha statues line a wall in the Banbullah temple, Sri Lanka. Buddhism has a great many dedicated teachers, each transmitting the Dharma *to the best of their abilities.*

During the life of the Buddha, many of his disciples attained enlightenment in his presence. They fully eradicated the fires of greed, hatred and delusion and, having attained nirvana, were released from *samsara*, the endless cycle of rebirth (see pp.72–3). These "worthy ones" (*arhats*) form part of the Noble Sangha (in which Buddhists take refuge, along with the Buddha and the *Dharma*; see p.80), and represent the ideal of the Theravada tradition (see p.78). Because they received the teaching as disciples, rather than discovering it for themselves, they are not "perfect" Buddhas.

Famous *arhats* include Sariputta, known for his wisdom and ability to teach; Moggallana, renowned for his mental and meditational power; and Ananda, the Buddha's attendant, who was recognized for his devotion and memory in reciting the Buddha's teaching at the First Council. Ananda is also known for his role in establishing the order of nuns.

Some 200 or 300 years after the Buddha's death, a new variation of the Buddhist ideal began to emerge. Dissatisfied with the seemingly limited goal of the *arhat*, this new vision emphasized the *bodhisattva* as the highest aspiration for all. A *bodhisattva* is a being who resolves to become a fully enlightened Buddha and who dedicates his efforts to helping other sentient beings to attain salvation. These compassionate beings figure predominantly in the Mahayana tradition (see pp.78–9); indeed, the most distinguishing feature of Mahayana Buddhism may be its advocacy of the *bodhisattva* as the vehicle to liberation.

The *bodhisattva* follows a long and arduous path, often described as having ten stages and spanning many lives, at the end of which he attains complete Buddhahood. The Mahayana is thus able to consider a host of *bodhisattvas*, at different stages along the path, as intervening in the lives of sentient beings. An advanced *bodhisattva*, for example, can create "Buddha Fields" (see p.79), to which humans can aspire to be reborn by devotion and righteousness.

The notion of the *bodhisattva* is at times combined with the doctrine of the "Three Bodies" of the Buddha (*trikaya*). This theory maintains that the ultimate form of Buddhahood and the true nature of things is the "Body of *Dharma*" (*dharmakaya*) itself. The Body of *Dharma* is revealed progressively by two other "bodies" (*kayas*): the "Enjoyment Body" (*sambhoga-kaya*), a subtle form perceptible only to those advanced in the path, and the "Transformation

AVALOKITESHVARA, THE *BODHISATTVA* OF COMPASSION

Avalokiteshvara, the "Lord Who Looks Down" on us with compassion, is one of the most popular Mahayana *bodhisattvas*. Revered as the embodiment of compassion, he is frequently depicted with eleven heads and 1000 arms, all of which are used in his dispensation of aid. Avalokiteshvara is an attendant of the Buddha Amitabha, who rules over Sukhavati, the Pure Land of the West. Amitabha is one of the most important of the many Buddhas who reside in the different "Buddha Fields" of Mahayana Buddhism (see p.79). Avalokiteshvara finds many ways to help, not least by assuming a variety of forms, including those of a disciple, a monk and a god. Tara, an important female *bodhisattva* in Indo-Tibetan Buddhism, was born from a teardrop of his compassion, and the Dalai Lamas (see p.91) are sometimes said to be successive reincarnations of Avalokiteshvara.

The cult of Avalokiteshvara has inspired some of the most beautiful works of religious art in Buddhist Asia. This 10th-century Chinese painting shows the bodhisattva *with only ten arms. Four of these hold the sun, moon, a mace and a trident; and the remaining six are in the distinctive gestures (*mudra*) of giving, banishing fear and offering.*

Body" (*nirmana-kaya*), a physical form apparent to all. According to this scheme, Gautama was merely a Transformation Body, an apparition of ultimate Buddhahood. Other *bodhisattvas*, who are Enjoyment Bodies, can also teach and intervene through transformation and apparition.

Important Mahayana *bodhisattvas* include Avalokiteshvara (see above); Manjushri, who personifies great wisdom (*prajna*) and is often represented holding a sword, which he uses to cut through the veil of ignorance; and Maitreya, "The Kindly One", who will be the next Buddha and who, after attaining Buddhahood, will send the next Transformation Body to teach on earth.

Other great Buddhist teachers are sometimes associated with *bodhisattvas,* and are even seen as their incarnations. One of these is Nagarjuna, who was an abbot at the Buddhist university of Nalanda in the 2nd century CE. Nagarjuna is considered the founder of the Madhyamaka, a school of Buddhist philosophy that was active in Buddhist India. Madhyamaka greatly influenced certain forms of Chinese and Japanese Buddhism (such as Zen) and still flourishes today in Tibet.

ZEN AND JAPANESE BUDDHISM

Of the many different forms of Buddhism practised in Japan, Zen seems to be the most familiar
to a Western audience, even though it accounts for
fewer than ten percent of contemporary Japanese
Buddhists. Perhaps it is the "artistic" side of Zen that
has appealed to Western sensibilities, or perhaps it is
its apparent directness and humour that have
enchanted a culture weary of religious complexity.
Part of the West's fascination with Zen lies in the
manner in which it was presented as an intelligible
and communicable way to talk about supreme (religious) enlightenment, a way that has "a sense of
beauty and nonsense, at once exasperating and
delightful", as Alan Watts (1915–1973), an important Western commentator, has explained. There is
no doubt that Zen has had a great influence on
Japanese culture: its ethics and technique were
adopted by samurai warriors and by practitioners of
the martial arts, its simplicity inspired haiku poetry,
its appeal to nature and beauty inspired architecture
and drawing, its serenity found expression in the tea
ceremony and its spirit is preserved also in the Noh
theatre. However, there is more to Zen than this, and
more to Buddhism in Japan than Zen.

Introduced to Japan in the 6th century CE by the
Koreans, Buddhism was welcomed by the Japanese
ruling class as a means of stabilizing and civilizing a
country that was torn by strife and feud. For the next
five centuries, it was predominantly the preserve of
the aristocracy and enjoyed increasing royal patronage, notably during the Nara period (710–84CE),
when the emperor Shomu built national temples
throughout the country. The dominant Buddhist
sects during this time, which included Tendai (see
right), were all forms of Chinese Mahayana, based
on Indian traditions. On the other hand, Zen, which
entered Japan from China in the 12th century, is
characteristically Japanese in its evolved form.
Unlike other prominent schools of Japanese
Buddhism, Zen is a monastic tradition: it extols neither *sutras* nor devotion but emphasizes meditational
and ethical discipline.

The name "Zen" is derived from the Chinese word
ch'an, which in turn is derived from the Sanskrit
dhyana (in Pali, *jhana*), meaning meditational
absorption (see p.77). Zen traces its origins to
the monk Bodhidharma (in Japanese, Daruma;
*c.*470–453CE), who later carried the tradition to

The monastery of Eihei-ji, set in the mountains on the Japan Sea, northeast of Kyoto, was founded in 1244CE by Dogen (see p.88) and has always been the most important centre of the Soto Zen sect. The monks there awake at 3 a.m. and meditate for hours every day, pursuing the path to gradual enlightenment. Their routine also involves manual labour, which is characterized by ritual action. Even in the washroom (right), they follow a strict procedure. Dogen taught that enlightenment can be found in action as well as in meditation.

TENDAI AND PURE LAND BUDDHISM

In 805CE, some two centuries after the introduction of Buddhism into Japan, the monk Saicho returned from China with a new form of Buddhism called Tendai (in Chinese, *T'ien-tai*). This sect focused on the teaching of the *Lotus Sutra* (see p.83) as the final and complete teaching of the Buddha. From its inception, Tendai has been eclectic, absorbing both the meditative practices of *ch'an* and the more esoteric teachings derived from Tantra. It also positioned itself at the hub of Japanese Buddhism, establishing Mount Hiei, near Kyoto, as the monastic and academic centre of its time. Generations of influential monks have obtained their training at the Enryaku-ji temple at Mount Hiei. Tendai still accounts for one-third of Japanese Buddhists today.

A different kind of Buddhism developed during the Kamakura

The popular Amida Buddha is shown seated at the centre of his Pure Land in this 18th-century Japanese woodblock print.

period (1185–1333). The savage fighting that ushered in this time convinced many that the dire age of *mappo* (last days) had begun. As a result, indigenous forms of Japanese Buddhism evolved that appealed to all classes, including the common people, who had previously been ignored. Among these was the Buddhist sect Jodo-shin, or "True Pure Land", a form

of Mahayana (see pp.78–9) that was established as a means for all to achieve salvation in *mappo*. Jodo-shin became a powerful feudal and military force in Japan around the 15th century, and is still active in the country.

Jodo-shin focuses primarily on Amida (in Sanskrit, Amitabha), the Buddha of Jodo, the "Pure Land". This Pure Land is a place for heavenly rebirth and, according to Jodo-shin, anyone can reach it merely by reciting the name of Amida. Everything else is considered redundant, including monastic practice, the common factor that holds together other forms of Buddhism (see p.78): Jodo-shin priests can marry and have children. Jodo-shin is fundamentally different from other forms of Buddhism, but it is still Buddhist by virtue of its spiritual and cultural origins.

China. Bright red Bodhidharma dolls are sold in Japan every new year. They have no legs because, according to legend, Bodhidharma sat so long in meditation that his legs fell off. It is also said that Bodhidharma cut off his own eyelashes as a penalty for falling asleep while meditating, and that tea plants later grew from these clippings.

There are two distinct schools of Zen in Japan, both of which originated from the teaching of monks whose lineages have been traced to Bodhidharma and, ultimately, to the Buddha himself. Rinzai Zen, founded by Eisai (1141–1215) at the

end of the 12th century, is best known for its use of the *koan*. A *koan* is a "riddle" with no apparent answer, and it is used to train the mind to obtain enlightenment (*satori*) in a sudden flash. Out of context, *koans* may seem too absurd to be of any use, but in context, they form an essential part of Zen training. Consider the sound of two hands clapping, suggests one famous *koan*. What, then, is the sound of one hand clapping? Such problems are put before Zen students by their masters. A student may spend years (or a split second) contemplating the meaning of a *koan*. When the master is satisfied with the pupil's reply, he will present him with another *koan*. The *koan* guides a person into seeking new interpretations, and it is said that "solving" a *koan* involves a mental leap. Zen is the gate to enlightenment, and the *koan* is the guide; however, in the words of one famous *koan*, "as there is no gate, come, let me tell you how to cross it".

The second form of Zen, Soto Zen, was founded by the great master Dogen (1200–1253). Advocating a simple life for both monks and laity, Dogen taught a form of meditation called *zazen* ("sitting meditation"), through which enlightenment could be attained gradually, instead of in an instant, as taught by the Rinzai school. Dogen is one of the most prominent religious figures in Japanese history. His philosophical writings are fundamental to Zen thought, and the monastery he founded, Eihei-ji, is an important Zen centre to this day (see p.86). Soto Zen shows reverence for *sutras* and for the exemplary life of the historical Buddha, Siddhartha Gautama. Stressing discipline, self-control and meditative practices, Soto Zen is perhaps the more "philosophical" and artistic of the two Zen schools.

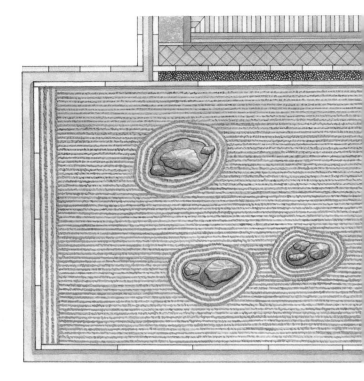

There are many stories concerning the rigours of Zen training. For example, it is said that when a pupil of Sengai, an outstanding 19th-century Zen master and painter, requested to leave Sengai's school, he received a whack on the head from the master. Whenever the young monk repeated his request, he would be whacked again. The pupil eventually solicited the aid of an elder monk, who spoke to Sengai and received his assurance that he would allow the pupil to leave. However, when the pupil went to thank his master, he received another whack. The elder monk asked Sengai if this meant that he had changed his mind about letting the young monk leave. "No", replied Sengai, "that was merely a parting whack because I know that this pupil will attain enlightenment, and when he comes back I will not be able to whack him again."

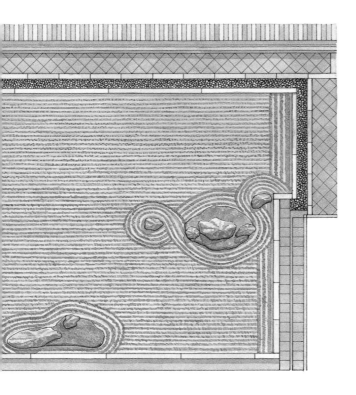

In its unique interpretation of Buddhist practice and principle, Zen transforms the garden into an aid to meditation. Influenced without doubt by the Japanese reverence for nature (see p.153), these gardens range from the simple to the lavish: a pond next to a cliff is the extent of Kamakura's Zuisen-ji, while lush trees, moss and a pond almost disguise the arrangement of boulders in the corner of Kyoto's "paradise garden" at Saiho-ji.

The abstract rock garden at the Ryoan-ji temple in Kyoto, illustrated here, is a world-famous example of the "dry landscape" garden form. Consisting of fifteen rocks arranged in groups on a bed of raked gravel, and surrounded by an earthen wall, its origins are unknown, although it has been attributed to the 16th-century painter and garden-artist Soami. Its meaning is also a mystery, inviting meditation and interpretation.

The plan of the garden (top left) shows the arrangement of the fifteen rocks, but this view would never be apparent to a visitor to the site. From any one point on the garden's perimeter, only fourteen of the fifteen rocks can be seen: a slight shift in position reveals a new rock, while one of the old ones slips out of sight.

Many interpretations have been offered of this deceptively simple garden, ranging from a tigress swimming with her cubs to islands in a sea. David Hockney's photo-collage (bottom left) reveals the complexity of the question. Only by piecing together a series of pictures of the garden, taken in succession at different points along the viewing platform, is he able to show it in its entirety. Slow and methodical deliberation can lead to sudden enlightenment in the Rinzai Zen tradition.

BUDDHISM IN TIBET

Buddhism was first carried to Tibet by Indian missionaries in the 7th century CE, but its influence waned after two centuries of political and religious turbulence. Reintroduced in the 11th century, it has since been at the centre of Tibetan society and culture.

Tibetan Buddhism is a form of Mahayana (see pp.78–9), and embraces a wide variety of schools and practices. On the one hand, its highly ritualized and esoteric character is derived from Indian Tantra, a form of "mystical" Buddhism which incorporates both Buddhist and Hindu ideas. On the other hand, its systematic and elaborate monastic culture has been influenced by the scholarly traditions of India.

The development of Buddhism in Tibet was greatly influenced by two figures, Padmasambhava and Atisha. A wandering Tantric yogi, an expert in magic and a master of the occult, Padmasambhava was called in by the king to help lay the foundations for the first Tibetan monastery at Sam-yay in the 8th century CE. He managed to subdue the local demons who had been foiling the project, and to put them in the service of Buddhist *Dharma*. He also established the Nyimg ma pa (*rNying ma pa*) Order, which is one of the four principal schools of Tibetan Buddhism. As both a great Tantric yogi and the founder of a monastic order, Padmasambhava symbolizes the two great trends in Tibetan Buddhism and is revered to this day. The same can be said of Atisha (982–1054CE), who came to Tibet in 1042CE. Atisha was a well-travelled Bengali scholar-monk, known throughout India for his erudition. He insisted on monastic discipline, emphasizing the importance of celibacy in the Sangha, but he also brought new understanding to the study and practice of the *sutras* and of Tantra. He stressed the cult of the *bodhisattva*

Avalokiteshvara (see p.85) and the importance of conventional Buddhist ethical practices.

Several other teachers (*lamas*) were active in Tibet during this period, each incorporating and blending different teachings. Over time different schools evolved, famous for their rivalry over spiritual – and at times political – supremacy. This diversity gave rise to a flourishing Buddhist tradition that has always been creative. Tibetans have mostly sought to integrate the different teachings into a coherent whole, and this has led to a proliferation of commentaries and other material, which have been well preserved alongside the classical *sutras*. The Tibetan version of the Buddhist canon was completed by the 14th

Hanging prayer flags, such as these in front of the Potala Palace, is one way to accrue merit in Tibetan Buddhism.

THE DALAI LAMA

Since the 17th century the Dalai Lama has been the ruler and spiritual leader of Tibet. Succession is by reincarnation, and after the leader's death his successor is sought and usually recognized in a young boy. Until adulthood, an appointed regent takes his place. All Dalai Lamas have a special relationship with Avalokiteshvara (see p.85): some maintain that they are reincarnations of the compassionate *bodhisattva*, while others say that they that are emanations of him, or humans blessed by Avalokiteshvara.

The 14th Dalai Lama has been in exile since 1959. His portrait hangs in a monastery in Gansu, China.

century and, because Buddhism in India had been destroyed at the end of the 12th century CE (see p.56), this has become one of the most important sources of Buddhist scriptures.

In the 16th century the Geluk (*dGe lugs*) Order, popularly known as the "Yellow Hats", gained the support of the Mongol rulers of Tibet, overcoming both the king and the competing Karma-pa Order. In the 17th century the Mongols installed the fifth Dalai Lama (1617–82) as the undisputed master of Tibet, and since then complete political control over

Tibet has been in the hands of the religious establishment. Until the middle of the 20th century, the Dalai Lamas were based in Lhasa, the Tibetan capital, where they ruled from the Potala Palace, located on the legendary abode of Avalokiteshvara.

In 1950 the Chinese army invaded Tibet, asserting China's territorial rights. Through colonial rule, and especially during the Cultural Revolution (1966–72), the Chinese sought to wipe out Buddhism in Tibet, destroying around 6000 monasteries. Many Tibetans have found refuge in India and Western countries.

CONFUCIANISM

Confucianism is a body of moral teachings that originated in China in the 6th and 5th centuries BCE. Based on institutions and practices that had long been current among the Chinese, such as the kinship system and its associated ancestor cult, it became the most influential system of thought in China, coexisting for centuries with Daoism and Buddhism. Its founder, Confucius (551–479BCE), was a political reformer and educator who became dissatisfied with the moral decline of his time and sought to revive the values of what he considered to be a Golden Age of antiquity. His philosophical, ethical and religious ideas underlie a universal system of morality, which has survived the test of time.

Confucius lived during the Zhou Dynasty (c.1027–256BCE), but by his time the Zhou kings had become mere figureheads. Real power resided with the aristocratic rulers of various principalities, who constantly sought to strengthen their positions and enlarge their domains at the expense of their neighbours. Confucius travelled from state to state trying to find a ruler sympathetic to his ideas, but his counsel was repeatedly rejected. Eventually he returned to his native state, Lu, and devoted himself to teaching.

Although he was unsuccessful as a politician, Confucius was without question a great teacher. The school of philosophy that he founded is called the *Ru* school: *ru* came to mean moralists or scholars. He claimed to be only a transmitter of tradition, not an innovator, but nevertheless he originated many of the core ideas

In this 16th-century lithograph, Confucius instructs three followers from the banks of a river. He wished to strive unceasingly for perfection, like a river which never stops flowing.

在川觀水

夫子在川觀見水子貢

that have sustained Chinese civilization for more than 2000 years. These ideas are contained in *The Analects of Confucius*, a somewhat disjointed account of his conversations compiled by his followers not long after his death. In spite of its formal imperfections, *The Analects* has been described as the most influential book ever written in East Asia. From China its message was spread to Korea, Japan and even farther afield.

In the 4th and 3rd centuries BCE, Confucianism was expanded by two major *Ru* philosophers, Mencius and Xun Zi, but during this time it did not occupy the dominant position that it would later enjoy. As one of the so-called Hundred Schools of Thought, it competed for influence with, among others, the Moists, who advocated universal love; the Daoists, who believed in the natural order and opposed the Confucians' moralizing; and the Legalists (Realists), who placed the interests of the state above all else. The Legalist doctrine was espoused by Qin Shi Huang, the First Emperor, whose armies unified China for the first time in 221 BCE, ushering in the imperial age. The Qin ruthlessly suppressed the Confucians, but the dynasty lasted only fifteen years and the next dynasty, the Han, elevated Confucianism above all other schools, making it the state cult. During the Han Dynasty, Confucianism became established as the basis of Chinese education, a position it held until the beginning of the 20th century.

The collapse of the Han at the end of the 2nd century CE and the ensuing period of chaos brought about a temporary decline in the fortunes of Confucianism. It was challenged in succeeding centuries by both Buddhism and Daoism, which provided a spiritual dimension to people's lives that Confucianism failed to supply. The Confucians responded by launching several revivalist movements in the Tang and Song dynasties (7th–13th centuries CE), with resounding success: the movement known in the West as "Neo-Confucianism", expounded by Zhu Xi (1130–1200), was accepted by the state as the orthodox doctrine throughout the long-lasting Ming and Qing dynasties (14th–20th centuries).

After the establishment of the Republic of China in 1912, there was a brief attempt to have Confucianism written into the constitution as a state ideology. This provoked a vigorous protest movement from young intellectuals, who viewed the tradition as an obstacle to political and economic modernization. The Communist movement was even more opposed to Confucianism, again regarding it as an enemy of progress. In recent years, however, the Chinese government has become more tolerant, mainly because of Confucianism's close links with the family system and its emphasis on social order and discipline. Today, although most of the institutions of feudal and imperial China have been swept away, the teachings of Confucius continue to exert an influence on the hearts and minds of the Chinese people.

CHINA IN CONFUCIUS' DAY

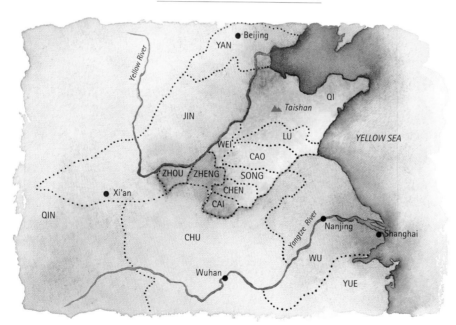

KEY

▪ States visited by Confucius, according to *The Analects.* (His visit to Zhou was recorded by a later Zhou tradition.)

● Modern cities

▲ Sacred mountain

In the 6th and 5th centuries BCE, when Confucius lived, "China" was made up of self-governing states, shown above, which battled for supremacy. (The word "China" derives from "Qin", the dynasty that united the area in 221 BCE.) Confucius tried to influence the rulers of states, but his ideas were not adopted by governments during his lifetime.

CONFUCIUS, THE GREAT MASTER

In this Chinese engraving Confucius is shown with one of his followers. Several disciples accompanied the Master on his journeys, and some achieved fame as scholars and teachers during his life and after his death.

Confucius (551–479BCE), one of the great thinkers in Chinese history, is known above all as a teacher. He accepted his first students at the age of thirty, and once said that he would teach anyone who came to him with the school fees of ten pieces of dried meat and who would perform the ceremony required for entering. He taught that in education there are no class distinctions, and he was the first person to spread education beyond the confines of the aristocratic class. His pupils, who probably came mostly from the professional class like himself, eventually numbered hundreds or even thousands. It was said that he had seventy-two disciples, but only about twenty-five have been reliably identified by name.

Confucius was born and lived most of his life in Lu (see map, p.95), one of the smaller principalities, situated in present-day Shandong Province. His Chinese name was Kong Qiu and he was called Kong Fu Zi (Master Kong). His name was latinized in the late 16th century by Jesuit missionaries. The earliest surviving biography of him is in Sima Qian's *Historical Records*, written around 100BCE, nearly 400 years after his death. This account contains legends that had accumulated over the centuries, many of which had no basis in fact. Most of what is known for certain comes from *The Analects of Confucius*, while other information is contained in the *Zuo Zhuan*, a commentary on the chronicles of the state of Lu, covering the period of Confucius' life.

According to the *Zuo Zhuan* and the *Historical Records*, Confucius' father was a strong man who once held up a portcullis with his bare hands to enable his comrades to escape. Nothing is known about his mother. As a child Confucius was fond of learning and, like his contemporaries, he studied the so-called Six Arts: ceremonies, music, chariot driving, archery, writing and arithmetic. He developed an interest in ceremonies and music, and hoped to serve as an official in the court of the Duke of Lu. His ambition was to restore to government the values and rites of the early Zhou Dynasty (see p.99).

Confucius was eventually appointed Minister of Justice of Lu, but soon fell out of favour. In 497BCE he left Lu and embarked on a journey that lasted thirteen years and took him to several of the principalities in what is now northern China (see map, p.95). He tried valiantly to convince the leaders of states to accept his advice, but his efforts were largely frustrated. In time he returned to his native Lu, where he abandoned his political ambitions and devoted himself entirely to teaching.

Although honoured as a sage in later times, and perhaps even during his own lifetime, Confucius never made such extravagant claims for himself. He once said that there was no hamlet of ten houses that could not produce men as loyal and dependable as himself. The one quality he did lay claim to was his love of learning and teaching. He was willing to learn from anyone, saying that in any group of three people there must be one from whom he could learn something. When one of his disciples was asked what kind of man Confucius was, he did not know how to reply. He asked the Master (Confucius), who said, "Tell him that Confucius is a man who is tireless in learning and tireless in teaching. When inspired he even forgets to eat."

Confucius was a moralist, but he was not a fanatic and did not demand perfection. He was delighted if his students made an effort to understand his ideas and demonstrated some progress. He was capable of great joy and great sorrow. When he heard the Shao music in the state of Qi, he did not notice the taste of meat for three days: he never dreamed that music could bring such joy. When Yan Yuan, one of his most accomplished disciples, died young, he wept uncontrollably. Others suggested that he was overdoing his grief, but Confucius replied, "Overdoing it? If not for him, for whom should I overdo it?"

Once, when Confucius was with four of his followers, he asked what they would most wish to do if a prince recognized their merits and gave them the freedom to act as they pleased. One said that he would like to be in charge of a small state surrounded by powerful enemies. Another said that he would like to control a district of about 500 square miles (1295 sq km): he would make it prosper within three years. The third disciple said that he would like to be a minor official assisting with the ceremonials in the royal Ancestral Temple. The fourth disciple, Zeng Xi, said, "In late spring I would like to take five or six adults and six or seven youths to bathe in the River Yi, and after bathing go to enjoy the breeze in the woods by the altars of Wu Yi, and then return home, singing as we go." Confucius sighed and said, "You are a man after my own heart."

In Confucius' time, most schools were run by the governments of states for the sons of aristocracy. The curriculum consisted of ceremonies, music, archery, chariot driving, writing and arithmetic (the Six Arts). Archery contests, such as the one shown in this late 18th-century silk painting, were considered essential training for combat. Warfare was conducted in a ceremonial way, by tournaments between warriors in chariots, although by Confucius' time warfare was becoming less civil.

THE FIVE CLASSICS

Confucius' teaching was based on six classic books: the *Yi* (*Changes*), *Shi* (*Odes*), *Shu* (*History*), *Li* (*Rites*), *Yue* (*Music*) and *Chun Qiu* (*Springs and Autumns*). Four of these were dignified by the word *jing* (classic) – *Yi Jing*, *Shi Jing*, *Shu Jing*, *Yue Jing* – and the six books became known as the Six Classics. In the 2nd century BCE, because the *Book of Music* had been lost, the five remaining books were renamed the Five Classics.

In *The Analects* Confucius mentions both the *Book of History* and the *Book of Odes*. The former is an assorted collection of official documents, mostly dating from the early Zhou Dynasty. They were of little interest to Confucius, and he did not refer to them often. The *Book of Odes*, however, was his constant companion. He must have known it by heart and could probably sing it. He mentioned it or quoted from it twenty times in *The Analects*. The *Book of Odes* contains 305 songs, including dynastic hymns which were sung at the Zhou court and folk songs from different parts of the Zhou empire. According to tradition, the king sent emissaries far and wide to collect folk songs, so that he could learn what people thought of his leadership.

Confucius recommended the *Book of Odes* to his students for several reasons. First, it would help them to understand the customs of the various states.

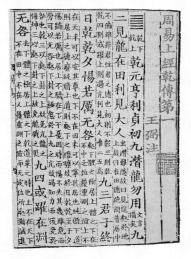

A page from a 10th-century woodblock edition of the Yi Jing *(I Ching), one of the Five Classics.*

Second, it would teach them to live harmoniously with other people: from the *Book of Odes* they could learn to better serve their fathers and the king. Third, it would be an outlet for their emotions. Finally, it would introduce them to foreign birds, beasts, plants and trees. Many of the odes are love songs, but Confucius put a moral gloss on them. He said, "If ... I were to select a phrase which expresses their meaning, it would be: 'Do not swerve from the path.'"

The *Book of Changes* (*Yi Jing*, or *I Ching*) is a manual of divination which came from the Zhou court and was later expanded by Confucian scholars. By manipulating sticks made from yarrow stems, sixty-four hexagrams can be produced, corresponding to all the structures and changes in the universe. The calculations that were involved in deciphering the hexagrams stimulated the development of mathematics and science in China.

No book of rites survives from Confucius' time. However, the *Li Ji*, which contains early Zhou material but was in fact compiled later, was given classic status. This book affirms the importance of ritual but also brings it up to date. For example, in the early Zhou period when a ruler died, his officials and concubines might be killed and buried with him so that their spirits could accompany him after death. This practice had long been abandoned, but it was still the custom to bury precious possessions with their owners. The *Book of Rites* denies that such spirit objects could be of use to the dead and recommends that crude imitations be used instead. These would sufficiently fulfil the purpose of the ritual, which was to express the feelings of the living for the dead.

The *Springs and Autumns* (*Chun Qiu*) records the daily, monthly and seasonal events in Confucius' state of Lu. The surviving parts cover the years 722–481 BCE. According to a later tradition, Confucius compiled the *Springs and Autumns* himself and edited the other classics. There is no evidence for this, but his association with the Five Classics greatly enhanced their prestige.

THE SAGES OF ANTIQUITY

In his teaching, Confucius looked back to what he considered to be the Golden Age of the past – namely, the age of peace and harmony at the beginning of the Zhou Dynasty (*c.*1027–256BCE). He had the greatest respect for the early Zhou kings, who had ordered the feudal hierarchy and devised the rites and music that he venerated. The rulers of his day were distorting and misusing these traditions, and in his travels Confucius tried to convince them to follow the models set by these and other ancient sages. His unsolicited advice was largely ignored.

The Zhou people came from the northwest and were once a vassal state of the Shang Dynasty (*c.*1523–1027BCE), the first historical dynasty. King Wen of Zhou, the "Civilizing King", built up the strength of the Zhou state until it was able to challenge the Shang; King Wu led the conquest of Shang; and King Wu's brother, the Duke of Zhou, established and consolidated power over the China of his time. In Confucius' eyes these three worthies could do no wrong, but the one dearest to his heart was the Duke of Zhou. The Duke was probably responsible for inventing the theory of the Mandate of Heaven (see p.100), by which the Zhou kings justified their conquest of the Shang, and he also had a special place in the rituals of the state of Lu. He was so important to Confucius as a model of the perfect ruler that the Master once said, "I am

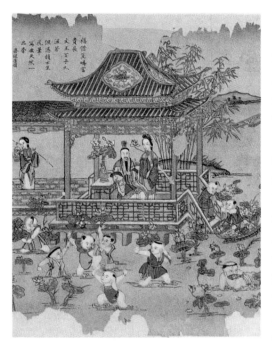

A 17th–18th-century woodblock print of King Wen, the "Civilizing King", one of the founders of the Zhou dynasty, watching children playing among lotus flowers.

slipping; I have not dreamed of the Duke of Zhou for a long time." The Duke of Zhou embodied the humanity and perfect moral order that Confucius preached.

In *The Analects* Confucius expressed his admiration for other sage kings who had lived in an age far more remote than that of the early Zhou. The two he mentioned most often were Yao and Shun. According to Chinese tradition, they lived in the 3rd millennium BCE, when China was ruled by a succession of emperors of outstanding virtue. Yao was a humble man whose primary concern was the welfare of his people. He lived frugally in a thatched cottage and ate simple food. When the time came to give up his throne, he did not consider his own sons to be worthy, and searched for a true sage to succeed him. He selected Shun and after a probationary period of three years, felt confident that he could abdicate in Shun's favour. Shun was a good judge of character and delegated many powers to his subordinates. It was said that he only had to sit on his throne and face south and the whole empire would be at peace. Shun eventually abdicated in favour of Yu, known as "Yu the Great", a heroic figure who was most famous for taming a flood. Another sage king, Yu is said to have founded China's first dynasty, the Xia, in the 20th century BCE. His supposed tomb still stands near present-day Shaoxing in Zhejiang Province.

HEAVEN AND THE SPIRITS

The image of the dragon, shown here on an embroidered fabric, was adopted by Chinese emperors as a sacred symbol of imperial power, which they believed to be mandated by Heaven.

The first ancestor of the Zhou people was Hou Ji, the god of millet, but the god they worshipped above all others was Tian (Heaven). They believed that Heaven ultimately decided the destinies of all beings in the universe, and that all human institutions were established in Heaven's name. When the Zhou overthrew the Shang Dynasty in *c.*1027BCE, this was deemed to have come about because Heaven decided that the Shang king was bringing harm to his people and therefore transferred its mandate to rule the empire to a more worthy successor.

This theory by which the Zhou justified their conquest of the Shang is known as the Mandate of Heaven, or Heaven's Decree. It is similar in some respects to the European Divine Right of Kings, with the refinement of an escape clause, which justifies conquest or rebellion to oust an oppressive ruler. Furthermore, the Mandate of Heaven makes the well-being of the people, not god, the prime consideration in Heaven's decision to transfer its mandate.

Originally, the Mandate of Heaven applied uniquely to the emperor or king: only he was entitled to offer sacrifices to Heaven at the appropriate times. This tradition persisted until the end of the last dynasty, the Qing, which was overthrown by the Republicans in 1911. In contrast, Confucius believed that the mandate's ethical sanction applied to all of society, and that everyone was duty-bound to live a moral life as Heaven intended. The idea of a moral universe persisted in Confucianism to modern times. The challenge for the individual was to comprehend Heaven's way. This was not an easy task: even Confucius, with all his learning and moral cultivation, confessed that he could not fully understand Heaven's decrees until he reached the age of fifty.

A short passage in *The Analects* suggests that Confucius believed that his own moral powers were endowed by Heaven. When he was in the state of Song (see map, p.95), it seems that his life was in danger from the local minister of war, Huan Tui. The Master said, "The power that is in me came from Heaven, so what have I to fear from Huan Tui?" This

The Temple of Heaven in Beijing is a reminder of the long tradition of imperial sacrifices to Heaven, which was discontinued in 1911. The brightly coloured roof-beams shown here support the Imperial Vault of Heaven, which was first erected in 1530 to portray the geometric structure of Heaven, as conceived by the architects of the Ming Dynasty.

implies that Heaven could not let Huan Tui kill Confucius without frustrating its own purpose. It was unusual for Confucius to claim abilities or powers above other people. Nevertheless, his reverence for Heaven is beyond doubt: "He who sins against Heaven has none to whom he can pray."

Confucius' concern with morality and human society was challenged in his day by a pervasive belief in ghosts and spirits. Rulers at that time believed in the prophetic nature of dreams and the significance of portents and prodigies, and divination was practised in the courts of every state. Confucius felt compelled to divert attention away from such fixations

with the supernatural and toward the problems of the living world. In a famous passage from *The Analects*, often quoted to support the notion of Confucianism as an agnostic doctrine, he berates his disciple Zi Lu for asking about the worship of ghosts and spirits. Confucius said, "You still do not know how to serve men, how then can you serve spirits?" When Zi Lu asked about the dead, Confucius replied, "You still do not know how to serve the living, how can you serve the dead?" Confucius did not deny the existence of spirits, but he believed that a gentleman should concern himself first and foremost with the study of humanity.

THE QUALITIES OF A GENTLEMAN

In *The Analects* Confucius described himself as a transmitter of tradition, not an originator. He wanted his disciples to become rounded men rather than specialists and he taught them different branches of knowledge based on the classic books (see p.98). His teachings went far beyond book learning, however, because the books were often obscure and Confucius had to interpret them in the light of his own moral concepts.

In addition to transmitting the cultural tradition of the past, which he viewed as the basis of stability (see p.106), Confucius originated new ideas to satisfy the intellectual and spiritual needs of his time. For example, he reinterpreted the words *junzi*, which meant a prince or ruler and, by extension, a member of the ruling class, and *xiao ren*, meaning small men or common people. Confucius used these terms frequently in *The Analects*, but usually in the sense of people exhibiting superior or inferior moral standards, as one might use the words gentlemanly and ungentlemanly. He said, "Gentlemen associate with others but do not form cliques. It is small men who form cliques," and, "The gentleman is calm and at ease, the small man is anxious and ill at ease." A gentleman was not necessarily a member of the aristocracy, although he might have been. He was primarily a man guided by high moral standards.

For Confucius, the supreme virtue of a gentleman, from which all others sprang, was *ren* (humanheartedness; also translated as benevolence or goodness). *Ren* has been described as the sum total of virtues, because Confucius once said that endurance, fortitude, simplicity and reticence are all close to the meaning of *ren*. When one of his disciples asked him how to practise *ren*, he replied, "Love people".

Ren is at the core of the ideal human relationship. It is closely connected with *shu* (reciprocity), in the sense that a man of *ren* judges others by the same standards that he sets for himself. Confucius expressed this principle in the so-called "Silver Rule": "Do not do to others what you do not wish done to you." Elsewhere he made the same point positively: "The good man is one who, wishing to sustain himself, sustains others, and, wishing to develop himself, develops others. To be able to use one's own needs as an example for the treatment of others is the way to practise *ren*."

Confucius denied that he himself had attained *ren*: "How dare I say that I am a sage or a man of *ren*? But I delight in striving toward *ren* and never tire of teaching what I believe." Still, he did not suppose that *ren* was entirely beyond men's reach. His young disciple Yan Yuan, at whose death he grieved so uncontrollably (see p.97), apparently achieved this great virtue: at his grave Confucius remarked that Yan "did not violate the principle of *ren* for as long as three months".

For Confucius it was self-evident that the sage rulers of antiquity, such as Yao and Shun and the Duke of Zhou (see p.99), possessed *ren*. He hoped that the leaders of his time would strive for it, even if they could not attain it. One of his disciples asked him: "Suppose a ruler is generous toward his people and helps them when they are in difficulty, would you say that he is a man of *ren*?" "He certainly is," replied Confucius. "He is not only a man of *ren*, he is a sage, better even than Yao and Shun." Needless to say, the rulers of Confucius' home state, Lu, fell far short of the standards of the legendary emperors that Confucius revered, as did those of the other states.

Another virtue that Confucius emphasized was *yi* (righteousness). This did not have any religious connotation, but rather meant doing what is morally right and proper in any situation, with special regard

to the Five Relationships upon which society was believed to be based: those between sovereign and subject, father and son, husband and wife, elder and younger brother, and friend and friend. *Yi* is often contrasted with *li* (in this context meaning profit or advantage, as opposed to rites; see p.106). While *ren* is the inner quality of goodness in the gentleman, *yi* is its outward manifestation in action, by which his character may be judged.

Filial piety (xiao; see p.115) is one of the most common ways in which Confucian ethics have been expressed over the centuries. Books on this subject recount how dutiful sons and daughters went to extraordinary lengths to make their parents happy. In this illustration from an edition of a Chinese collection of moral tales, The Twenty-Four Examples of Filial Piety *(compiled in the 14th century), subjects pay homage to their king, as a child would to his or her parents.*

TOP "Juniors should be respected."

BOTTOM "If you do not give a thought to the distant future, you will be in trouble when it comes near."

TOP "Is it not a pleasure to have friends come from afar?"

BOTTOM "To learn without thinking is fatal but to think without learning is just as bad."

TOP "When three people walk together, there is sure to be one from whom I can learn."

BOTTOM "Rule by the power of moral example."

TOP "He who is impatient over trifles will make mistakes in major enterprises."

BOTTOM "Do not do to others what you do not wish done to you."

A selection from The Analects of Confucius

CONFUCIAN RITUAL

As a student of the Six Arts (see p.96), Confucius specialized in ceremonies, which were traditionally conducted by the court and by aristocratic families. In his teaching he expanded the notion of ritual so that it involved all levels of society. Rites (*li*) were important to Confucius because they were handed down from the Golden Age of the past. He believed they could civilize human behaviour and provide a framework for the ordering of society. Such practices as ancestor worship (see right), mortuary rites and sacrificial ceremonies served to reinforce the five formal relationships between people. In addition, some Confucians viewed rites as a way of pleasing or influencing Heaven, the deities or ancestors.

Confucius and his followers took ritual seriously at all levels, even applying it to a person's bearing and attitude in everyday situations. The *Book of Rites* (see p.98), for example, contains instructions on household management as well as extensive passages on sacrifices and mourning rites. However, the Confucians were primarily concerned with state ritual, because this affected all of society. Confucius believed that true kings had power bestowed on them by Heaven (see p.100) and that they were able to retain their authority by enacting kingly rites. He taught that the welfare of the state and its population depended on the correct performance of these rites. This was how the sages of antiquity were able to govern successfully.

By Confucius' time, although there was still a Zhou Dynasty king, none of the rulers of states obeyed him, indicating that he had forfeited Heaven's mandate. The state rulers could claim only a fraction of the authority of a king, yet they were performing ceremonies appropriate to true kings. For example, the Ji family, which had usurped power in Lu, had eight rows of dancers perform in their courtyard, something that only the Son of Heaven was permitted to do. To Confucius this was a symptom of serious moral decline, requiring immediate action.

Although the practice of ritual in China was for many years suppressed by the Communists, it continued to thrive in other places that were affected by Confucianism. Some east Asian countries celebrate September 28th as Confucius' birthday. In South Korea, the day is an official holiday known as "Teachers' Day", and is celebrated with ceremonies such as the one shown here, from the Chonghyo Shrine in Seoul.

ANCESTOR WORSHIP

The Chinese have long believed in the existence of the soul after death. Ancestors are thought to watch over the living, but they must be given the love and respect of their descendants in order to ensure their attention. This belief has found expression in the ancestral ceremonies observed by family and clan.

Ancestor worship existed before Confucius, but as a matter for the court, not for the general public. Confucius popularized the practice, teaching that it could strengthen family ties and play an important role in ensuring the continuity of the family. Confucian said that the most unfilial behaviour of all is not to have descendants, not only because this is a mark of disrespect to your parents, but also because it means that there will be nobody to burn incense to you when you eventually become an ancestor yourself.

The simplest ancestral ritual consisted of burning incense and bowing every morning and night before an ancestral portrait or a wooden tablet bearing the ancestor's name. On the anniversary of the ancestor's death, and on other important occasions, such as festivals, more elaborate ceremonies were enacted. Each family member would kowtow (bow until the head touches the ground) before a tablet or portrait of the deceased or, in the case of festivals, before a portrait of the ancestor who was regarded as the family's founder. The head of the family performed the rite first and others followed in order of seniority.

In addition to burning incense, the family might burn paper money to provide for the spirit's needs, and place offerings of food and drink in front of the altar. After reciting prayers, they would invite the ancestors to partake of the nourishment, although usually the living family would consume it in the end.

More elaborate ceremonies were organized by the clan, which was composed of all the families of one surname living in a town or district. Clan temples existed for this purpose. Like the family, the clan relied on ancestor worship for the maintenance of unity and continuity. The most important clan

A portrait of Mao Tse Dong hangs in a small family shrine. The altar holds incense and family portraits, and the central inscription dedicates the shrine to Heaven, Earth, Earthly Rulers, Ancestors and Teachers.

ceremonies were held at the spring and autumn equinoxes, at the start of the growing season and after the harvest.

Although for many years the Communists suppressed all types of ritual in China, there has recently been a resurgence of ancestral activity. Most families in the countryside have a small ancestral shrine in their houses where simple rites are enacted, and richer families, especially in the south, may have separate buildings for this purpose. In Taiwan, Hong Kong and overseas Chinese communities, where there has been less political disruption of traditional customs, ancestral rites are also practised.

MENCIUS AND XUN ZI

According to legend, Mencius' mother moved house three times in order to provide her son with a better learning environment. When he would not do his lessons, she broke the thread on her loom to teach him the importance of diligence: his lifestyle would suffer if she did not finish her weaving. This scene is portrayed here on a 17th–18th-century woodblock print.

In the two and a half centuries after his death, Confucius' ideas were embellished and complemented by two other philosophers of the *Ru* school: Mencius, who lived in the 4th century BCE, and Xun Zi, who lived in the 3rd. Both taught Confucian ethics and strove for political reform, claiming that the ruler who followed the Confucian model would be the great ruler of China. Yet they had to compete with rival schools of thought that had not existed in Confucius' day, and they developed ideas of their own to meet the requirements of a new era.

There are several legends about Mencius' early life, but few reliable facts. The best source of infor-

mation about him is the *Book of Mencius*, which is second only to *The Analects* in importance among Confucian texts. The *Book of Mencius* was probably compiled some time after Mencius' death, although it may contain some of his own writings. It gives more contextual information than *The Analects* and is less disjointed, and therefore can be used as a supplement to the earlier book.

Like Confucius, Mencius came from the state of Lu and visited a number of states offering advice that was inevitably rejected. He also criticized two main opponents of Confucianism. One was the philosopher Mo Zi (479–*c.*380BCE), whose school was as influential as the Confucians up to the 3rd century BCE. Mo Zi attacked the Confucians on a number of issues: for not believing in the gods and spirits; for advocating wasteful expenditure on ceremonies and music, such as a three-year mourning period after the death of a parent; and, above all, for supporting a hierarchical society in which there was discrimination. Mo Zi believed that the evils of the world resulted from favouring one's own family, clan or state over others. He advocated universal love as the standard for everyone.

Mencius also opposed an early form of Daoism that was represented by a shadowy figure called Yang Zhu (dates not known). Yang supposedly said that he would not sacrifice one hair of his body to benefit the world. This may have been a distortion of what he meant, but nevertheless the Daoist belief in *wu wei* (non-action; see p.122), clashed with the Confucian emphasis on ritual and reform.

Criticizing these two schools, Mencius said, "Yang Zhu's principle of 'each for himself' is like abolishing the sovereign, while Mo Zi's principle of 'universal love' abolishes fatherhood. To have no sovereign and no father is to be like the birds and beasts." Mencius did not believe that it was possible for people to love their neighbour's children as much as their own. He taught that a person can extend love to those who are distant only if he or she loves those who are near. Such distinctions are necessary for the proper functioning of society.

Mencius is best known for his theory of human nature. He taught that humankind is inherently good and that a person need only look inward to discover the source of morality in his or her heart. If a ruler did this, people would flock to him "like water rushing downhill" and his state would prosper.

Xun Zi, who was born around the time that Mencius died, took the opposite point of view. "The nature of man is evil; his goodness is acquired," he wrote. "Only when people are influenced by teach-

ers and laws and guided by rites and morality can courtesy be observed and order maintained."

Xun Zi lived in times that were very different from those of Confucius or even Mencius. Developments in commerce and technology, such as the use of iron, had created new possibilities for growth and enrichment, particularly in the larger states. After centuries of warfare, the smaller states had been swallowed up and around a half dozen powerful states remained. Under these circumstances Xun Zi could not accept Mencius' idealistic view of human nature, nor did he believe that Heaven was the sole arbiter of human behaviour. He asserted that the importance of humankind in the universe is equal to but different from the importance of Heaven and Earth: "Heaven has its seasons, Earth has its riches and Man has his culture. This is what is meant by the Trinity." Humanity's function is to utilize the resources of Heaven and Earth to create its own culture. This can be done through the strength acquired from social organization. However, because social organization needs to be regulated, lest it break down, and because "desires are many, but things are few", Xun Zi taught that people need to be restricted and guided by rules and morality.

Both Mencius and Xun Zi stressed the importance of education, as Confucius had done, but for different reasons. Mencius believed it could draw out what was already present in people in an inert state, while Xun Zi viewed it as a chance to instil morality into the young in their own and society's interests.

While Mencius has been described as a representative of the idealist wing of Confucianism, Xun Zi, while still retaining some of Confucius' basic concepts, was more of a realist. He was in tune with the times to the extent that two of the minds behind the Qin conquest of 221BCE (see p.110) were Xun Zi's students. In later ages, however, it was the *Book of Mencius* that was accepted into the Confucian canon. Xun Zi never quite achieved Mencius' status.

THE STATE CULT

Before it was established as the state cult, Confucianism survived ruthless suppression by the Qin Dynasty (221–206BCE). The First Qin Emperor, shown in this late 18th-century painting, ordered Confucian books to be burned and scholars to be executed.

When the state of Qin unified China in 221BCE, it ended the era in which various schools of thought contended for political influence. The First Qin Emperor, Qin Shi Huang, supported the Legalist (Realist) school, which advocated the concentration of power and wealth in the hands of a centralized state. He was anxious about the recently conquered states making a comeback, and wanted to extinguish any opposition to the Legalists by the Confucians, Moists and other schools that had previously enjoyed prestige. His ambitious prime minister, Li Si, who had been a student of Xun Zi (see p.109), advocated banning all competing schools and burning their books, except for those copies held by imperial professors, and works on agriculture, divination and

medicine. This order was to include the Five Classics (see p.98), as well as the histories of rival states.

The Qin emperor accepted Li's recommendations and in 213BCE issued an order for them to be carried out. Anyone failing to comply would have his face branded and be sent to the frontier to build the Great Wall. However, in spite of these draconian measures, there were books that escaped the net, including some of the classics, which were found many years later hidden in a wall of Confucius' old house. Also, the Chinese often learned their classical books by heart and were able to reproduce them when the fifteen years of Qin tyranny were over.

Although the Qin rule was excessively harsh and repressive, it succeeded in breaking the power of the old hereditary aristocracies by establishing a system whereby officials were appointed on the basis of their contribution to the state, rather than by hereditary rank. It also divided the country into administrative regions, the governors of which were appointed by the centre. This was the beginning of the unified bureaucratic monarchy, which would rule China for 2000 years.

The Qin Dynasty was succeeded, after a brief period of political chaos, by the Han Dynasty (202BCE–220CE), in which Confucianism became the state doctrine. The Han emperors continued to operate an administrative system similar to that of Qin, but permitted the re-emergence of the different philosophical schools that had been suppressed by the previous dynasty. They soon realized, however, that they would need a single system of thought in order to govern such a large and diverse area.

In 136BCE the Han Confucianist Dong Zhongshu presented a memorial to the throne in which he advocated making Confucianism the basis of the state. He suggested that all people who wished to be considered for an official position should have to study Confucianism and the Five Classics, but he did not go so far as to recommend banning the non-Confucian schools or punishing their adherents. The Han Emperor Wu Di accepted Dong's proposal, and in 124BCE an academy was established in the capital, Chang'an, for aspiring officials to study the Confucian classics. Candidates for entry into the academy were selected on the basis of recommendation, which was then reinforced by examination. Succeeding dynasties expanded and refined this system until entry into government service through examination on the classics became the norm rather than the exception. The system was abolished in 1906 as part of an attempt to modernize education, and a Western style of examination was introduced.

THE WORSHIP OF CONFUCIUS

During the Han Dynasty there were several attempts to make people believe that Confucius was more than a philosopher and teacher. Dong Zhongshu claimed that after the decline of the Zhou Dynasty, the Mandate of Heaven (see p.100) had been bestowed not on the Qin or Han dynasties, but on Confucius. He used the text of the *Springs and Autumns* (see p.98) to justify this unusual hypothesis, claiming that the book was an important statement of Confucius' political policies, which he made as the rightful king. This theory was believed by other members of Dong's school, and they went to great lengths to explain it.

During the 1st century BCE, some Han Confucians started composing new texts, which they claimed were missing components of Confucius' opus. Known in the West as the apocrypha, these books were given considerable credence at the time, although they were later recognized as forgeries. The most extravagant of these documents stated that Confucius

The Confucian temple in Nanjing, the city on the Yangtze River which was the capital of China for short periods.

was the son of a god called the Black Emperor, and that he had the power to foretell the future and perform miracles. The book's author also claimed that Confucius had predicted the coming of the Han Dynasty.

The worship of Confucius as a god dates from this period, although many Confucian scholars protested against such extravagant claims, reasserting the view that Confucius was neither a king nor a god, but a sage. Nevertheless, over the centuries Confucian temples were built in many parts of China. The first of these was established by the state of Lu in Confucius' birthplace, Qufu, in modern Shandong Province.

During the Tang Dynasty (618–907CE) Confucian temples were extended by imperial decree to all major cities throughout the land. Local governors had to go and pay their respects to the Master at the temple before taking up their appointments. Ceremonies were conducted there annually, and the temples became especially connected with education and the examination system (see above): lists of successful candidates for the civil service were carved on stone steles in the courtyard of the Confucian temple in Beijing. Such temples survive today not only in China but also farther afield, in Korea and Japan.

NEO-CONFUCIANISM

An early 20th-century painting of a Vietnamese schoolroom, where pupils would have read the Neo-Confucian classics.

Following the collapse of the Han Dynasty in 220CE, there was a prolonged period of disunity, caused first by the failure of any single Chinese warlord to unite the country and then by invasions of non-Chinese people from the north and northwest.

The emperor Kang Xi (1662–1723) became an able Chinese scholar and patron of Neo-Confucian learning.

During this time, and in the ensuing Sui and Tang dynasties (581–907CE), Buddhism and Daoism developed as religions in China, gaining a mass following among the people and also enjoying considerable imperial patronage. Confucianism lost much influence, although it continued to be the official philosophy of the court and bureaucracy. In particular, the Buddhist notion of karma (the law of moral retribution; see pp.72–3), entered the popular psyche, bringing comfort to many who suffered hardship in those troubled times. The Confucians had attributed inexplicable events to the working of Heaven or Fate, but the Buddhists indicated that suffering was due to a person's bad behaviour in a previous existence. They also taught that good behaviour would be rewarded by happiness in a future incarnation.

There was a Confucian revival among scholars in the Tang Dynasty, but it was not until the Song Dynasty (960–1279CE) that Confucianism regained its popular status. Unlike the Tang philosophers, who had opposed Buddhism, the Song Confucians incorporated important elements of both Buddhism and Daoism into their theories. Known in the West as Neo-Confucianism, the new movement dominated Chinese thought until modern times.

Neo-Confucianism is known to the Chinese as the School of *Li*, although in this case *li* does not mean ritual (see p.106), but rather principle or reason. The concept of *li* was expanded and developed by the greatest of the Neo-Confucian philosophers, Zhu Xi (1130–1200). Zhu explained that before the world and its myriad objects were created, their principle already existed. For example, there was a *li* of boat building before anyone thought of building a boat. Human nature is the *li* of humankind and, like Mencius (see pp.108–9), the Neo-Confucians believed that this is innately good. Zhu Xi compared humankind's *li* to the lustre on a pearl, saying that just as a pearl loses its shine when it is covered with dust, so the goodness of people is tarnished by earthly passions. The wise will try to free themselves from these passions by extending their understanding of the world.

The *li* of the universe is an all-embracing principle called *Tai Ji* (Supreme Ultimate), which Zhu Xi described as comprising the *li* of Heaven and Earth and all things. However, *li* alone is not sufficient to explain the universe, because *li* is "above shapes" (i.e., abstract). Zhu Xi introduced another principle, *qi*, to explain the physical universe, or what is "within shapes". *Qi* is the material or instrument by which things are produced. One type of *qi* has received the principle of movement and is called "yang"; the other has received the principle of quiescence and is called "yin". The interaction between yin and yang produces the Five Elements – metal, wood, water, fire and earth – of which all things are composed.

Neo-Confucianism owes a great deal to Buddhist and Daoist thought. Its emphasis on subduing

Following the colonization of parts of North Korea by the Chinese during the Han Dynasty, Korea has maintained close connections with China. The Korean Yi Dynasty (1392–1910) embraced the Chinese system of government, adopted Neo-Confucian ethics and installed the Four Books (see below) as the basic texts of education. Korea's continuing respect for Confucianism is attested to by the South Korean national flag, shown above, which includes the yin and yang symbols and the trigrams of the Yi Jing.

worldly passions is in accord with Buddhist practice (see pp.76–7), and its Supreme Ultimate is superficially akin to the *Dao* of the Daoists (see pp.121–2). However, the Neo-Confucians' basic aim was to improve society rather than escape from it, so philosophically they were still significantly different from the Buddhists and the Daoists.

The Neo-Confucians' ideas broke new ground in the history of Chinese philosophy, but their effect on social progress was not so positive. Like their predecessors, they viewed society as being based on the formal relationships between sovereign and subject, father and son, husband and wife, elder and younger brother and friend and friend (see p.103). They taught that the *li* of these relationships was immutable: thus, any fundamental social reform was regarded as contradicting the natural order. In the Yuan, Ming and Qing dynasties (1276–1911), their word became writ and was used by successive regimes to obstruct intellectual and social progress.

The cornerstone of the new orthodoxy was the Four Books, which became the basic texts of Chinese education for centuries. The Four Books are *The Analects of Confucius*, the *Book of Mencius*, *The Doctrine of the Mean* and *The Great Learning* (the two latter works are in fact chapters from the ancient *Book of Rites*). Zhu Xi wrote commentaries on these classics and also presented many of his ideas in plain, easy-to-understand vernacular Chinese in the form of recorded conversations with his followers. Later Neo-Confucians revered Zhu Xi to such an extent that they established a succession of sages from Confucius to Mencius to Zhu Xi.

CONFUCIANISM TODAY

In China, Confucian reverence for ancestors can still be seen at the annual Qing Ming festival on the 5th of April. Here, a group gathers at a family graveyard in south China to clean the graves, burn incense and make offerings of food.

Confucianism profoundly affected the structure and values of Chinese society for 2000 years. The majority of Chinese officials were Confucians, or at least strongly influenced by Confucianism. This was also true of the landowners and gentry who controlled the countryside, and the heads of guilds, clans and families. It is impossible to discuss such institutions as the monarchy, the central and local bureaucracy and the clan and family separately from the Confucian ideas that moulded and sustained them.

The Confucians viewed the Chinese social system largely in family terms. The sovereign was revered as the father of his subjects, while the district magistrate, the emperor's representative, was often referred to as the father and mother of the people. In theory, the social relationship was considered to be two-sided: the Mandate of Heaven would be withdrawn if the emperor did not take good care of his subjects. In practice, however, the system was heavily weighted in favour of those in authority. This bias spurred on the young intellectuals who led the anti-Confucian

movement in the 1910s and '20s. They believed that Confucianism, with its overwhelming respect for the elderly, stifled the spirit of enterprise and forced women into a state of permanent subjugation. They also argued that the Confucian nostalgia for a long-lost Golden Age held back social progress. These ideas attracted increasing numbers of young people.

During the complicated and fierce military and political struggles that have characterized 20th-century Chinese history, Confucianism has become somewhat marginalized as an ideological issue. The New Life Movement, introduced into Chinese cities during the Second World War by Chiang Kai-shek and Madame Chiang, attempted to impress upon the young such Confucian values as altruism, courtesy and modesty, but to little effect. It was soon swept away by the powerful Communist movement, which rejected the authoritarian and backward-looking teachings of Confucianism. Nevertheless, many aspects of Confucianism were still tacitly accepted: the concept of dedicated public service, the care for the aged, the idea that a government stands or falls by its treatment of the peasants and the ideal of loyalty, for example. Other aspects of Confucianism are still very much in evidence. Respect for the aged continues to play a major part in Chinese politics, and the paternalism exhibited by many east Asian organizations, in both government and industry, owes much to 2000 years of Confucian influence. The tradition's emphasis on education is still reflected in the importance attached to it by east Asian parents; and within schools, the students' respect for teachers parallels filial piety within the family, creating a learning environment which is more disciplined than that of most Western countries.

THE CHINESE FAMILY AND FILIAL PIETY

The Chinese have been predominantly farming people for over 3000 years, and their family structure was devised to ensure the family's continuity and to maintain its connection with the land. The ideal was an extended family with four generations living under one roof. The line of inheritance passed from father to eldest son, and authority resided with the patriarch. He would control all external dealings, while his wife would usually be in charge of internal family business. Younger generations deferred to their elders, and within generations the older had precedence over the younger.

The Confucians placed great emphasis on the family as a moral training ground. They believed that qualities bred in the family would transfer to the outside world, where the social system was seen largely in family terms (see left). Filial piety (*xiao*) was seen as the cornerstone of family order: a child owed loyalty and respect to his or her parents, just as a subject did to his or her sovereign. Confucius himself did not speak much about filial piety, but it was important to Mencius (see pp.108–109), and from the 1st century BCE, it became a constant theme of Confucian writings.

In the 20th century, especially since the establishment of the People's Republic of China (1949), the Chinese family system has been transformed by rapid economic and social change. Industrialization led many people to break their ties with the land, and the collectivization of agriculture in the 1950s and '60s introduced new patterns of relationship, which to a certain extent supplanted kinship ties. In recent years the reintroduction of family-based farming units and the policy of restricting families to one or, in some cases, two children has created new problems. Families used to rely on sons to provide future security and family continuity, but now many are taking out insurance as an alternative provider. They are also making alliances with friends or distant relatives to give them economic strength. In this period

A Chinese family in Taiwan offers prayers to the goddess of the moon at the Mid-Autumn Festival. The act of ritual is seen as cementing family ties.

of uncertainty, there has been a revival of religious and ancestral activities (see p.107). Also, within the family basic values instilled by the Confucians continue to be honoured. For example, although freedom of choice in marriage is the declared policy of governments, it is rare that young people in east Asia do not take account of their parents' wishes.

DAOISM

Daoism has existed alongside Confucianism and Buddhism in China throughout the centuries, and has had a major impact on Chinese intellectual and spiritual life. As a philosophy it is in many ways the antithesis of Confucianism: Confucians concern themselves with people as members of society, while Daoists reject society and emphasize people's development as individuals. As a religion, which derived from the philosophy, it again diverges from Confucianism, embracing the spirit-world and the occult and minimizing Confucianism's emphasis on rituals and morality. Daoism has always provided a means of escape from the rigidity of Confucian orthodoxy, but in a wider sense Confucianism and Daoism reflect two sides of human nature. It is quite possible for a person to embrace both, one in work and family duties and the other in leisure and artistic pursuits.

According to tradition, Daoism was founded in the 6th or 5th century BCE by Lao Zi, who may have been a legendary figure. He is believed to have written the *Dao De Jing*, a book that has become the bible of Daoist thought. Daoism's central principle, the *Dao,* is a profound metaphysical concept which motivates and guides the whole universe. The *Dao De Jing* teaches that the way for the individual to achieve happiness and contentment is to seek oneness with the *Dao*, following the example of the natural world.

Daoism has always had its mysterious side, but by the 4th century BCE, when it began to emerge as an organized philosophy,

A Daoist priest rests by the Yangtze River in central China. His cap bears a rectangular piece of white jade – the stone is of special significance to Daoists and is a symbol of purity.

it was also concerned with problems of state. At the time, China consisted of a number of warring principalities, and the Daoists attributed this unrest to the rival governments, and to the attempts of these governments to instil morality into the people. Unlike the Confucians, who preached organization and regulation, the Daoists believed that the state should interfere as little as possible into the lives of people. They idealized a return to rural simplicity in which people would be content to conduct their affairs unconcerned about what went on in the next village.

The fall of the Han Dynasty in 220CE ushered in a period of political and economic chaos which lasted for almost four centuries. Confucianism, which had been closely connected with the state during the Han (see pp.110–11), became discredited, but Daoism developed as a religion during this time, attracting a mass following among the common people. Groups concerned with the occult, which had existed separately from Daoism in previous centuries, now attracted increasing numbers of Daoist followers, and the pursuit of immortality became a key aim of the religion. The Daoists also adopted many features from Buddhism, which had entered China from India in the 2nd century CE, developing its own priesthood, monasteries and temples, a pantheon and a canon of scriptures.

The Daoist religion reached its peak during the Tang, Song and Yuan dynasties (618–1368CE), when priests performed extensive social functions, such as aiding the passage of souls to the afterlife, healing the sick and exorcising demons. In recent centuries Daoism has gradually declined, owing in part to the impoverishment of its temples. Further blows to its survival were dealt in the 20th century by anti-religious movements. The most radical of these was Chinese Communism, which gained control over China in 1949. The Communists saw all religion as an obstacle to social progress and the Daoist religion in particular as harmful superstition. Since the early 1980s, however, the government has come to accept that for many people religion can fulfil real human needs, and a certain amount of tolerance has been restored. As a result there has been a resurgence of religious activity in the countryside. In towns, too, some of the larger Daoist temples are again functioning.

MAJOR RELIGIOUS SITES OF DAOISM

Some of the most important Daoist temples are situated on or near the summits of China's sacred mountains. The Daoists valued the mountains' solitude and also believed that mountain tops brought them closer to the sources of the Dao than anywhere else. Huashan (Mount Hua) in Shaanxi Province, Maoshan, near Nanjing in Jiangsu, Longhushan in Jiangxi and Wudangshan in Hubei are now the centres of major Daoist sects.

LAO ZI AND THE *DAO DE JING*

According to tradition, Daoism was founded by a man named Lao Zi, who may have been a contemporary of Confucius (551–479BCE). His life is steeped in legend. Even his name is a mystery, more likely an affectionate title than an actual given name: the literal meaning of Lao Zi is "old master", or "wise old man". Sima Qian's *Historical Records*, written at the beginning of the 2nd century BCE, contains a biography of Lao Zi which states that his given name was Li Dan. This account reports that Confucius went to visit him in the old Zhou dynasty capital to seek instruction on the rites. Lao Zi told Confucius that he sought the words of people who had long ago rotted with their bones, and that he should rid himself of lustfulness, arrogance and ambition. According to Sima Qian, Confucius was most impressed by Lao Zi's wisdom and compared him to a dragon riding on the wind.

Sima Qian also wrote that Lao Zi lived in Zhou, where he cultivated the Way and virtue and taught meekness. When he saw that Zhou was in decline, he decided to leave so that he could spend his final years in peaceful solitude. Mounting a water buffalo, he rode west, toward present-day Tibet. At the border he met the Keeper of the Pass who, sensing that Lao Zi was about to leave the world, asked if he would mind putting his beliefs in writing. Lao Zi sat down and wrote the book that came to be known as the *Dao De Jing* (the *Classic of the Way and its Power*). He then departed, and was never heard from again.

Sima Qian was writing several centuries after the time of Confucius, when these events are thought to have taken place. The pro-Daoist tone of his account of Lao Zi's meeting with Confucius suggests that he was repeating a Daoist story intended to promote the view that Lao Zi was senior to and wiser than Confucius. Most scholars agree that the name Lao Zi is to be taken in its literal meaning, and that the *Dao De Jing* was probably edited by someone who attributed it to a "wise old man". Nevertheless, Lao Zi continues to be venerated as the author of the *Dao De Jing* and founder of the Daoist tradition.

The *Dao De Jing* is the best known and most revered of all the Daoist classics. It is terse in style and consists largely of aphorisms, giving it an air of serenity and mystery. Over half of the book is written in verse, possibly so that it could more easily be learned by heart. Although it is credited to Lao Zi, it is more likely that it was compiled over a period of time and reached its final form around the 3rd century BCE, after receiving the attentions of more than one editor. Occasionally quite different or even contradictory aphorisms follow each other, simply because their subject-matter is the same. For this reason the *Dao De Jing* is more easily understood as an anthology of sayings with a common philosophical tendency, rather than as a book by a single author.

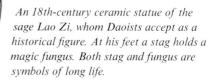

An 18th-century ceramic statue of the sage Lao Zi, whom Daoists accept as a historical figure. At his feet a stag holds a magic fungus. Both stag and fungus are symbols of long life.

THE WAY AND ITS POWER

While Confucius urged people to follow the commands of Heaven in order to become more benevolent and better members of society (see pp.100–101), Lao Zi urged them to model their behaviour on the way of nature, as encapsulated in the *Dao* ("Way" or "Path"). The complexities of interpreting the *Dao* become immediately apparent

The Chinese character for Dao.

in the first few words of the *Dao De Jing*, which state that the Way that can be spoken of is not the constant Way – that is, the *Dao* cannot be described in words. Nevertheless, there are aphorisms in the book that illuminate Lao Zi's meaning. First, the *Dao* is the principle that is responsible for the creation of all things: "From the *Dao* there comes one. From one there comes two. From two there comes three. From three there comes all things." Second, the *Dao* has such universality that it cannot be defined. It is like an uncarved block of wood: to classify it, to carve the block, would be to impair its completeness. Third, the *Dao* is associated with the Chinese term "non-being" (*wu*) rather than with "being" (*yu*): "All things in the world come into existence from being, and being comes from non-being." In other words, "All things are born from something and something is born from nothing." The "nothing" here refers to the *Dao*. Lao Zi compares the *Dao* to the hub of a wheel on which the spokes depend, to the empty space within a pot, without which the clay would have no function, and to the windows

The black and white yin–yang symbol, surrounded by the eight trigrams of the Yi Jing, *are shown on this park gate outside Bangkok. Daoists embraced these symbols as representations of the powers of the cosmos.*

and doors of a room, which likewise are composed of nothing.

The *de* in *Dao De Jing* is usually translated as "power" or "virtue". It is a quality that emanates from the *Dao*, and is manifested in the world of nature and in human beings. In Chinese cosmology two forces operate throughout the universe: yin and yang. Yang encompasses the qualities of brightness, hardness and masculinity, while yin represents darkness, softness and femininity. Confucianism is seen as a yang philosophy, because it believes in actively interfering in and guiding society toward its social and political goals. Daoism, on the other hand, is yin in spirit: passive, meek and content to leave things as they are. Its power comes directly from nature, and it can best be understood by following the way of the natural world.

Unlike the Confucian Heaven, the *Dao* of the Daoists is neither moral nor partial – it is like the laws of nature in this respect. Nature confirms the Daoist preference for the soft and hidden qualities of yin over the brightness and hardness of yang. Water in particular is considered to represent the *Dao*: "Nothing is softer than water, yet it is stronger than anything when it attacks hard and resistant things. Gentleness prevails over hardness; weakness conquers strength"; "The highest good is like water. Water benefits the myriad creatures without contending with them and comes to rest where none wishes to be. Thus it is close to the *Dao*."

The *Dao De Jing* teaches that the basic way to conform with nature is to practise *wu wei* (non-action). This does not literally mean doing nothing, which implies laziness and lack of thought, but rather not indulging in useless effort and not doing anything that contradicts nature – two actions which, in the Daoist view, will only lead to the opposite of the intended result. Thus, the *Dao De Jing* suggests that a sage or a ruler can achieve much by doing nothing in particular and can teach a great deal by remaining silent (see below). The people and the state will develop on their own, without external intervention: "Do nothing, and there is nothing that will not be done."

To Daoists, life is in a constant state of flux: nothing is fixed. The *Dao* has a moderating influence over everything and operates in a way that the *Dao De Jing* describes as fanning (reversal). If anything is pushed too far, it will be restored by the *Dao* to its previous condition – a notion that has some of the same implications as the "swing of the pendulum" often referred to in Western political commentary.

On a personal level, Lao Zi exhorts his readers to "hold fast to the submissive". This involves leading a simple life, free from the desires and ambitions that inevitably cause a reversal of fortune. In troubled political times, holding fast to the submissive might also enable a person to avoid an untimely death.

THE DAOIST STATE

Like other schools of thought that contended for influence in the Warring States period (see p.94), Daoism is a political philosophy. Although there never was an established Daoist state, the *Dao De Jing* has much to say about what such a state would be like. First, the ruler would interfere as little as possible with the lives of the people. Second, he would not attempt to educate them or preach to them, because education would increase their knowledge, and knowledge increases desire. He would simply ensure that the people had enough to eat and could live in peace. Naturally, he would avoid provoking or becoming involved in wars. The *Dao De Jing* explains: "The more restrictions and prohibitions there are in the world, the poorer the people will be. The more weapons people have, the more troubled the country will be. The more skilled craftsmen there are, the more pernicious contrivances will

The characters for wu wei *in the Beijing Imperial Palace indicate state endorsement of Daoist ideas.*

appear. The more laws that are made, the more thieves and bandits there will be."

Having eliminated the causes of discord and envy, the ruler would apply the principle of *wu wei* (non-action) to his task of government. The people would be like children, living in innocent simplicity: "If the people do not see anything to excite their desire, they will not be confused. The sage rules by emptying their minds, filling their stomachs, weakening their wills and toughening their sinews, so that they are without knowledge and without desire." The sage also aspires to simple innocence, but this comes as a result of self-cultivation, rather than from avoiding temptation. In the society of the time nobody suggested that all men are born equal.

ZHUANG ZI AND LIE ZI

The *Book of Zhuang Zi*, written in the 3rd century BCE, and the *Book of Lie Zi*, compiled some 500 years later, are, with the *Dao De Jing*, considered to be Daoist classics. Both are of uncertain authorship, and parts of the *Book of Lie Zi* might be derived from the *Book of Zhuang Zi*. Nevertheless, taken together they represent the continuing influence of philosophical Daoism through the 4th century CE.

The historian Sima Qian suggests that the *Book of Zhuang Zi* was written by a man called Zhuang Zhou, a contemporary of the philosopher Mencius (*c.*371–298BCE; see pp.108–9) who lived in the state of Song (in present-day Henan Province; see map, p.119). During Mencius' time this state suffered an exceptional amount of civil strife. Most commonly referred to as Zhuang Zi, the author of the so-called "inner chapters" of the book, which include the first seven chapters, was a considerable genius. Not only was he an original thinker, but he was also one of the most inventive and stimulating writers in Chinese literature. The *Book of Zhuang Zi* is full of witty and provocative anecdotes, which are expressed in vividly descriptive language.

Zhuang Zi's message is that if people wish to be free, they must cast aside the conventional values with which humankind has burdened itself and free themselves from the world. He does not mean that people should live apart from their fellow human beings, but that they should refrain from seeking fame or wealth and live in a state of *wu wei* (non-action; see p.122), in which their behaviour becomes as spontaneous as the natural world. Like Lao Zi he taught that every being is endowed with its own *de* (power), which derives from the *Dao*. The *de* is at the core of the human constitution, and people are happiest when the *de* is freely exercised, without external interference. To illustrate this point, Zhuang Zi

writes: "A duck has short legs, but if we try to stretch them it will feel pain. A crane has long legs, but if we try to shorten them it will feel distress." The same principle can be applied to human beings. The imposition of such institutional restraints as laws and codes of morality can only distort people's nature and frustrate their *de* – according to this logic, it is preferable to govern by the principle of *wu wei*.

Zhuang Zi bitterly criticizes rulers of states and preachers of morality. He cites the example of a robber named Zhi, who was once asked whether thieves have any virtues. Zhi replied, "To know where the valuables are hidden requires intelligence. To be the first to enter the house shows bravery. To be the last to leave the house requires righteousness. To know whether or not to enter a house requires wisdom. To divide the spoils equitably requires justice. It is quite impossible to be a great thief without possessing all five of these virtues." Zhuang Zi argues that because

ZHUANG ZI'S BUTTERFLY DREAM

Zhuang Zi teaches that everything is relative. What seems tiny to a human being will be gigantic to an insect; and what looks big will be insignificant compared to the universe. Even the states of dreaming and wakefulness must be taken in context, as illustrated by the following story.

Once Zhuang Zhou (Zhuang Zi) dreamed that he was a butterfly. He did not know that he was Zhuang Zhou. Suddenly he woke up and there was no doubt that he was Zhuang Zhou. However, he was unsure whether he was Zhuang Zhou who had dreamed that he was a butterfly, or a butterfly who was dreaming that he was Zhuang Zhou.

sages possess the same virtues as thieves, they do more harm to humankind than good.

According to Zhuang Zi, everything is relative, in both time and space. He viewed birth, life and death as part of the same natural process and refused to apply such adjectives as good and bad or desirable and undesirable to them. He compared life and death to the succession of day and night, and taught that they should not disturb a person's inner tranquillity.

The *Book of Zhuang Zi* refers to a certain Lie Zi, and it is possible that the author of the *Book of Lie Zi* borrowed this name from the earlier text. Certainly, because the *Book of Lie Zi* was compiled *c*.300CE, some 500 years after the *Book of Zhuang Zi*, any connection with the original character must be tenuous. The *Book of Lie Zi* does not possess the literary merit of the *Dao De Jing* or the *Book of Zhuang Zi*, but it is more prosaic and straightforward. Popular among the Chinese people, the stories in the *Book of Lie Zi* illustrate such Daoist ideas as the path of non-action, the relativity of values, the insignificance of humankind in a vast universe and the need for people to follow the laws of nature, rather than attempting to conquer them.

Like the *Book of Zhuang Zi*, the *Book of Lie Zi* contains many anecdotes, often concerning well-known figures of antiquity, such as Confucius and his disciples, whom the author usually treats as though they were apprentice Daoists, but sometimes openly ridicules. In one story Confucius is made to look foolish by two children. The author writes that when Confucius was travelling in the east, he saw two small boys arguing beside the road. One announced that he thought the sun was nearer at sunrise, the other countered that it was nearer at noon. The first child said, "When the sun has just risen it is as big as a chariot awning; by noon it is as small as a plate. Surely it must be nearer when it is big than when it is small." The second child answered, "When the sun rises the air is cool; by noon it is like dipping your hand into hot water. Surely it must be nearer when it is hot than when it is cool." Confucius could not decide which child was right. The two boys laughed and asked, "Who said you are a learned man?"

According to legend, Lie Zi had reached near-perfection and could ride about on the wind. This feat was often depicted in art, as in this detail from an early 17th-century wall panel from the Ryoan-ji temple in Kyoto, Japan.

FOUR IN THE MORNING AND THREE AT NIGHT

Like Zhuang Zi, Lie Zi warned people to beware of sages, because although sages profess a concern for others, they ultimately act in their own interests. To illustrate this point, he tells the story of a monkey-keeper named Zu Gong, who lived in the state of Song.

Zu loved monkeys and even understood their thoughts. He denied himself and his family food in order to feed his pets, but finally he began to feel deprived and was forced to cut the monkeys' rations. He was afraid that the monkeys would object, so he decided to trick them by using cunning.

"If I give you each three nuts in the morning and four in the evening, will that be enough?" he asked. When the monkeys jabbered in protest, he put forth a counter-proposal: "How about four in the morning and three at night, then?" The monkeys were pleased with this alternative and lay down quite satisfied.

The sages fool the people, cautions Lie Zi, just as Zu Gong fooled the monkeys.

THE SEVEN SAGES OF THE BAMBOO GROVE

Although Confucianism was officially the state cult (see pp.110–11) throughout the long-lasting Han Dynasty (202BCE–220CE), it was not the only influential system of thought in China. Both Daoism and Buddhism were developing during this period and attracted, in particular, the interests of the common people.

Confucian bureaucrats started losing their influence as early as the end of the 2nd century BCE, when the centralized Han state began to decay. Confucianism had become tainted by outside influences, such as beliefs in omens and in portents declaring that floods, droughts and pestilences were Heaven's punishments for the emperor's mistaken policies. The accusations against the emperors mounted, and eventually the Confucians were either killed or driven from the court. Even before the Han Dynasty fell, many intellectuals had turned to Daoism.

The leaders of the new Daoist movement were very different from the traditional Daoist sage, even though they drew their inspiration from Lao Zi (see p.120) and Zhuang Zi (see pp.123–4). Their dislike of conventions was manifested in their nonconformity. This was combined with a spontaneous and hedonistic lifestyle, as well as with a love of nature, which was more characteristically Daoist.

The earliest and most famous example of this trend was the group called the Seven Sages of the

The Seven Sages of the Bamboo Grove challenged Confucian etiquette and inspired creativity. The group is believed to have held its convivial meetings in a bamboo grove, as depicted in this 20th-century painting by Fu Pao-Shih.

Bamboo Grove (3rd century CE). Two of the sages, Ruan Ji and Ruan Xian, who were uncle and nephew, were great drinkers. When they met they drank from a large communal pot of wine, and when their pigs were thirsty, they would share the wine with the animals. However, the greatest drinker of them all, who became the Chinese god of wine, was Liu Ling. He rode about the capital in a cart, clasping a pitcher of wine to his bosom, and was accompanied by a man carrying a spade who had orders to bury him on the spot if he should die.

The Seven Sages are famous for their eccentricity, but there was method in their apparent madness. They sought to undermine the elaborate and stultifying Confucian code of conduct which had become a serious impediment to creativity. The Seven Sages were all creative artists. The most accomplished of them, Ji Kang, was a metal craftsman and a musician. His treatise on the lute is the earliest substantial work on a musical instrument in Chinese. He was also a famous poet and prose writer.

The Seven Sages initiated a period that saw the development of a new aestheticism, in which poetry, painting and music flourished. This continued through the 4th century CE, in which the great calligrapher Wang Xizhi and the pastoral poet Tao Yuanming lived, both of whom were strongly influenced by Daoist ideas.

ALCHEMY AND THE PURSUIT OF IMMORTALITY

During the 2nd century CE, many legends were circulating about Lao Zi. It was said that he was able to prolong his life through meditation and other practices, and that after leaving the Zhou territories in a cart pulled by a green ox, he had travelled with his disciple, the Keeper of the Pass, into the western lands (Central Asia) and converted the barbarians to Daoism. Among these barbarians was the Buddha.

With such an illustrious background, it is not surprising that Lao Zi was adopted by some of the many Chinese peasant cults as their patron. These early religious communities engaged in various forms of occultism, such as communing with the spirits of the dead, foretelling the future and healing the sick with spells and incantations. They also performed breathing and sexual exercises as a means of prolonging life. These activities stemmed from shamanistic practices, which were current among the population.

Daoism became associated with the occult around this time. In the 3rd century CE, the Daoist scholar Ge Hong revived the practice of alchemy, which had existed in China from the 2nd century BCE. Ge Hong rejected Zhuang Zi's idea that death should be accepted as part of the way of nature (see p.124). He declared that because life is so good, death should be delayed for as long as possible, and he encouraged

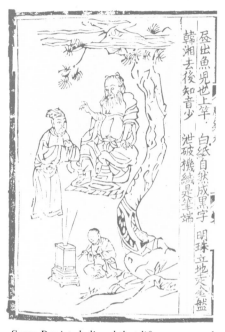

Some Daoists believed that life was so good that it should be extended forever. Experiments in alchemy, such as this one recorded in the 13th-century book Alchemy and Chemistry, *sought to discover the elusive elixir that could offer physical immortality.*

experiments to discover a medicine for prolonging life. As in previous times, alchemists aimed to produce gold from base metals. It was believed that gold, if absorbed into the body, should render the human form incorruptible, because gold itself was an incorruptible substance. Cinnabar (mercuric sulphide) was also widely used, but for the opposite reason: under certain conditions it underwent a dramatic change and became the liquid metal mercury. It was thought that cinnabar's propensity to change might stimulate change in other substances.

The Daoists did not confine themselves to chemical experiments, which they described as "external alchemy". They also indulged in "internal alchemy" in order to discover an elixir of life within the body. This involved breathing exercises, sexual exercises and meditation (see p.129). In addition they ate rare plants and fungi, which they believed could help them to live longer.

An important by-product of external alchemy was the advance it stimulated in Chinese science and technology. The blending of sulphur and saltpetre was recorded in the 4th century CE, and the addition of carbon to this mixture in the 9th century resulted in the invention of gunpowder. It is ironic that a technique intended to prolong life should have yielded such a potentially destructive product.

The crane, shown on this 18th-century embroidered surcoat, was a popular symbol of the Daoist quest for immortality. It was said that the crane had perfected life-prolonging techniques and could live for 1000 years.

DAOIST MEDITATION

In chapter six of the *Book of Zhuang Zi*, one of Confucius' disciples, Yan Hui, reported to the Master that he was making progress in meditation and that he had forgotten the distinction between goodness and righteousness. Later he said that he had forgotten rituals and music. Finally he claimed that he had forgotten himself while sitting. When Confucius asked him what was meant by forgetting oneself while sitting, Yan Hui replied, "It is to free oneself from bodily form and disregard seeing and hearing. Through the transcendence of bodily form and the elimination of sensations, one identifies oneself with the infinite." In this passage Zhuang Zi is presenting Confucius as an apprentice Daoist and suggesting that Yan Hui is his master.

The aim of Daoist meditation is to empty the mind of thoughts that are distorted by an individual's consciousness. This is called "sitting and forgetting". On a superficial level it may seem similar to Zen practices (see pp.86–8), but the Daoists' aims are different from those of the Buddhists. Daoists believe that the individual human being (the microcosm) is merely an external manifestation of the universe (the macrocosm). Both human being and cosmos share the three life-forces – spirit (*shen*), breath (*qi*) and vital essence (*jing*) – and in meditation the practitioner strives to join the microcosm and macrocosm into one. A first step in this process of unification is to rid the self of all dichotomous notions, such as those of good and bad, giver and receiver, and subject and object. The end-result is believed to be identification with the unitary origin of all phenomena – in other words, the *Dao* – which can ultimately reveal to the practitioner the secret of immortality.

In addition to meditation, which concentrates on the spirit, other practices focusing on breath and vital essence are alternative or complementary methods of achieving the same goal. Breathing exercises aim to coax the *Dao* from the atmosphere, while sexual experiments aim to stimulate and at the

Sima Chengzhen, the 8th-century CE *author of the* Zuo Wang Lun (Discourse on Meditation), *is shown "sitting and forgetting" in this 13th-century Chinese woodblock print.*

same time preserve the vital essence (*jing*). Sexual intercourse is regarded by Daoists as beneficial to both partners, but one way for the man to preserve his *jing* is to practise coitus reservatus.

Taken together, meditation, the control of breath circulation and sexual yoga comprise what is known as "internal alchemy", and an individual might practise all three. However, many Daoists believe that meditation alone can achieve the required result. Orthodox Daoists do not practise sexual yoga at all, preferring to concentrate on spiritual rather than physical processes.

閑來隱几枕書眠　夢入
壺中別有天　彷彿壺嶠
夷親面目大　還真訣得
親傳晉昌唐寅為
東原先生寫圖

In this intricately painted scene dating from the Ming Dynasty (1368–1644) the artist, Tang Yin, depicts himself dreaming of immortality in a thatched hut. The picture was painted for the artist's friend Dong Yuan and inscribed with a short poem by Tang:

"With my books as a pillow I fall asleep
and dream of another world within my wine jar;
my eyes can perceive the infinitesimal;
and the alchemic secrets are vouchsafed to me."

THE FIVE BUSHELS OF RICE SOCIETY

Toward the end of the Han Dynasty, many peasants were forced off the land by flood, famine and the increasing rapacity of warlords who had been emboldened by the collapse of central power. Many of these peasants joined Daoist religious communities (see p.127), which provided some sort of stability in a situation in which the official government organizations were in a state of collapse. These communities not only offered physical security against bandits and bullying landowners, but also provided moral support with their religious and magical doctrines. In due course, they came into conflict with the government authorities and were forced to fight for survival. Two major Daoist rebellions broke out almost simultaneously. The first was the Taiping Dao (The Way of Great Peace), led by Zhang Jue in present-day Hebei Province, north China (see map, p.119). This rebellion became known as the Yellow Turbans, after the colour of the headdress worn by its participants. Although it was the larger of the two rebellions, it was eventually crushed by a coalition of Han Dynasty generals who were forced to unite against their common enemy.

The second major Daoist-inspired movement, which arose in present-day Sichuan Province in the west of China (see map, p.119), is often identified as the forerunner of the Daoist religion. This was the Five Bushels of Rice Society, which was named after the contribution that each member was supposed to make to the common treasury. The society was led by Zhang Ling, later known as Zhang Daoling, whose power allegedly came from Lao Zi himself. It was said that Lao Zi visited him in a mountain cave, bemoaning the state of the world, and that he established Zhang Daoling as "Heavenly Master", commissioning him with the task of restoring the true Way. A charismatic figure who claimed to possess

magical methods of curing diseases, Zhang Daoling encouraged his patients to confess their sins and to pray to three divinities: Heaven, Earth and the *Dao*.

The Five Bushels of Rice Society succeeded in setting up a political regime that survived for two decades in parts of Sichuan and Shaanxi provinces. Daoist priests acted as officials, collected taxes and maintained the peace. Members were required to read the *Dao De Jing* and to follow its teachings by living simple lives and refraining from envy and avarice. They were also encouraged to carry out charitable acts, which included building roads and

caring for the sick and elderly. Hostels were established throughout the areas controlled by the society, and free rice and meat were given to travellers.

The Five Bushels of Rice Society won considerable respect, and early in the 3rd century CE, when the warlord Cao Cao established the Wei kingdom in north and central China, he allowed it to continue. By then Zhang Daoling's grandson, Zhang Lu, had inherited the leadership. In the 4th century CE, when China was split by the Hun invasions, the movement travelled south and continued to be influential among the people and leading statesmen of the time.

Harvesting rice near Dali in Yunnan Province. Rice was also the staple crop in Sichuan Province, where the Five Bushels of Rice Society originated. In China, it has always been the custom for farmers to pay taxes and rents in kind.

In 415CE a Daoist named Kou Qianzhi accepted the Five Bushels of Rice Society as a branch of Daoism and assumed the title of Heavenly Master, previously held by Zhang Daoling and his successors. The head of the Daoist religion has since used the same title, and is often referred to in the West as the Daoist "Pope". Today the Heavenly Master sect is one of four major Daoist sects in China (see p.143).

BUDDHISM AND DAOISM

Religious Daoism was profoundly influenced by the arrival of Buddhism in China in the 2nd century CE. Already a mature tradition, Buddhism had a well-established and highly sophisticated body of doctrine and a long history of religious observance, carried on not only in monastic institutions but also in temples at which the laity could offer incense and pray. It had an extensive literature and a large group of scholar-monks engaged in religious study. The Mahayana school (see pp.78–9), which predominated among the incoming missionaries, included in its hagiography not only the many incarnations of the Buddha, but also a host of other divinities, including *bodhisattvas* and *arhats* (see pp.84–5). This

DAOIST TEMPLES

The Daoists, like the Buddhists, were drawn toward the solitude of the mountains, which for them had religious significance, and Daoist temples stand on many of China's sacred peaks (see map, p.119). There is no specific Daoist architectural style, but many of the temples seem to represent physically the Daoist quest to become one with nature (see p.121), blending in unobtrusively with their surroundings.

Daoist temples are generally of two types. The smaller, privately owned temples are called *zisun miao* (inherited temples), and are run by Daoist masters who are eventually succeeded by their senior apprentices. These temples are allowed to accept novices for training, but are not permitted to ordain them as priests. They are the basic units of Daoism to be found throughout China.

The second type of Daoist temple is the *guan*, a word that originally meant "to observe". These larger temples are linked to the communities known as *Shi Fang Conglin* (Ten Directions Grove), whose name symbolizes the Daoist desire to draw strength from the universe: the "ten directions" refer to the eight points of the compass, as well as to above and below. *Guan* are either the collective property of the priests or the property of a Daoist sect. Their organization is complex and they may have up to twenty officers, most of whom are elected, in charge of various activities. All Daoist priests have the right to stay in a *guan*, but first they must undergo a test to confirm their credentials. These temples are authorized to carry out ordinations, but they do not accept novices, unless they have been recommended by the small temples (*zisun miao*). They also serve as Daoist centres in the main cities. The Baiyun Temple in Beijing belongs to this category.

An ancient Daoist temple stands in Jiangling, Hubei Province. Throughout history Daoist temples have fallen into disrepair, often as a result of local economic conditions. During the Cultural Revolution (in the 1960s and '70s), many temples were damaged or destroyed, but in recent years much restoration work has been undertaken.

introduced human imagery into Chinese religion for the first time. Amitabha Buddha (see p.79) took pride of place in most Chinese Buddhist temples, promising to lead all who chanted his name and believed in him to his Western Paradise. Guanyin, the goddess of mercy, who offered compassion to suffering humankind, was also revered.

For some Chinese people, the fact that Buddhism was an alien religion must have militated against its acceptance. Such concepts as reincarnation and karma (the law of moral retribution; see pp.72–3) must have been difficult to comprehend. But for the common people, who were pressed by famine, flood, pestilence and civil strife, the Buddhist message of salvation for all humankind was of decisive importance. The peaceful and solemn atmosphere of the Buddhist temples, the incense, and the chanting of the monks must have had a powerful effect on the lay worshippers who attended Buddhist festivals and ceremonies in increasing numbers.

Daoism, by contrast, was a new religion and lacked most of the trappings that attracted people to Buddhism. The Daoists responded to Buddhism's challenge by adopting many of their rival's institutions and establishing a priesthood, monasteries and temples (see left), a pantheon (see pp.138–9) and a corpus of sacred writings called the Daoist Canon, which was modelled on the Buddhist *Tipitaka* (see p.82). As Buddhism became more popular, Daoists began to celebrate festivals that were originally Buddhist, although they called them by different names. For example, on the fifteenth day of the seventh lunar month, the Chinese people carry out a ritual and communal banquet which is intended to release suffering souls from hell. This festival is Buddhist in origin, as is the concept of the hell from which the souls are to be released. However, on this occasion Daoist priests perform their own rituals, which, like their Buddhist counterparts, are intended to effect a general amnesty of souls.

This 12th-century Buddhist scroll shows proselytising Buddhist arhats *(saints) demonstrating the power of Buddhist* sutras *(see pp.82–3) before a group of Daoists, who can be identified by their black hats and black-trimmed robes. The* arhats *claimed that the* sutras *were the words of the Buddha.*

135

PRIESTHOOD AND RITUAL

*Senior Daoist priests and their abbot (centre) stand in front of a large temple (*guan*) in Qingdao, Shandong Province.*

Ritual and meditation are the two main forms of religious activity in Daoist monastic life, and in most Daoist sects, ritual, being a collective activity, is regarded as the more important. In this respect Daoism maintains the ancient Chinese tradition upheld by Confucianism, in which ritual is also of central importance (see pp.106–7). Many aspects of classical ritual are retained by the Daoists, such as the positioning of the high altar and the representations of the supreme deities in the north, so that the priest can conduct rites facing them. The difference between Daoist and Confucian ritual lies in the significance of the act. To some Confucians the act of ritual is of primary importance, and its effect on ghosts and spirits is secondary. The Daoists, however, strongly believe in the power of spirits, and regard ritual as an effective means of harmonizing human life with the forces of the universe.

To become an abbot, the head of a large Daoist temple (*guan*), a priest must pass rigorous tests and be a person of the highest integrity and reputation. The abbot's position is largely honorary, because his elected assistants oversee the running of the temple, but he does have the duty of performing ordinations. Priests rise in rank as they progress in mastering rituals and texts of the Daoist canon. Often the texts are so difficult that they must be clarified by a teacher, and these teachings must also be learned.

The priests' day starts at 5am with the tolling of the temple bell, and this is followed by the cleaning of

ABOVE *Daoist priests often place paper money on the tablet in front of a tomb. The spirit of the deceased can use it to make life easier in the other world.*

LEFT *Burning incense in the Wong Taisin temple, Hong Kong. Daoists believe that the smoke of incense can carry prayers up to the gods.*

the temple. The assembled priests then chant a series of incantations concerned with purification. After breakfast, which is followed by further incantations, the abbot's officers attend to their duties; the rest of the priests study either alone or with their teachers, or engage in Daoist exercises. Some temples chant incantations at noon and again in the evening, while others perform this ritual only in the evening. On certain days in the Chinese calendar, all religious activities are taboo to Daoists. The birthdays of gods and spirits, however, are celebrated as festivals, and elaborate sacrificial ceremonies are conducted. These may be preceded by purification ceremonies, which aim to empty the body of all evil so that it becomes more accessible to the *Dao*. The main ritual includes making offerings, burning incense and chanting

scriptures, and is accompanied by dancing and music. The hanging of banners that bear the pictures of the various gods and spirits associated with the occasion is also an important part of the festival.

In addition to their activities within the temple, Daoist priests perform social functions in the community, such as aiding the passage of souls to the afterlife, healing the sick and exorcising evil spirits. Because evils of all kinds are blamed on malignant spirits, Daoist priests are supposed to know which spirit is responsible for which particular evil and to apply the appropriate remedy, be it a charm, religious ceremony or medicine. Ordained Daoist priests are sometimes given a list of gods who come within their particular jurisdiction, so that they can work on cultivating a special relationship with these deities.

THE DAOIST PANTHEON

The Daoist pantheon developed over many centuries, gathering new deities as it branched out in different regions. In early Daoism, Heaven, Earth and the *Dao* formed a trinity (see p.132); and the mythical Yellow Emperor, supposed progenitor of the Chinese people, and Lao Zi (see pp.120, 127) also featured as objects of veneration. As religious Daoism developed, some of the various traditions cultivated the concept of the "Three Pure Ones", who were the personifications of the three life-giving spirits (see p.129): *qi* (breath), *jing* (vital essence) and *shen* (spirit).

A 19th-century image of a door god. Such paper figures were pasted on either side of entrances each New Year, to protect the building from evil spirits.

In later centuries the Jade Emperor became accepted as the head of the Daoist pantheon. He is first mentioned in written records dating from the 9th century CE, when there was a great expansion of Daoist influence in the imperial court. The ruling emperors of the Tang Dynasty (618–907CE) claimed to be descended from Lao Zi because they shared with him the surname Li. The Jade Emperor's status was boosted when he was accepted into the state pantheon in the 11th century CE, after an emperor claimed to have seen him in a dream. He became the senior member of a new Daoist trinity, and, together with his ministers and assistants, immortals and spirits, he controlled the spirit-world just as the emperor and his ministers controlled the physical world. His officials included a number of personified stellar deities, such as the Big Dipper constellation, whose position in the sky enabled him to look down on all people and report their activities to the judge of hell, who presided over the ten courts of hell, and decided their fate.

Other Daoist divinities included ancient culture heroes such as the creator goddess Nü Gua; the Queen Mother of the West, Xi Wang Mu, who presided over the abode of the immortals; geographical features, such as mountains and rivers; the planets and major stars, which were all personified; the patrons of various occupations, such as carpentry, acting and sailing; the spirits who supervised positive human activities (the state examinations), as well as negative ones (robbery, drunkenness and fornication); and various animals, such as dragons, tigers, snakes and crickets.

Daoism appropriated many of the ancient animistic deities, the worship of whom pre-dated both Daoist philosophy and Daoist religion, and it is difficult to identify a particular deity as being exclusively Daoist. This distinction is sometimes irrelevant, however, because Chinese religion is often practised in families and other social groups, rather than in institutionalized places of worship. For example, every Chinese household used to keep the image of the kitchen god in a special place. The god's duty was to observe the family's behaviour and to report to the Jade Emperor once a year. Every twenty-third day of the twelfth month of the lunar calendar, his lips

A 17th-century ivory carving of Shou Lao, the god of longevity. Also known as Shou Xing Gong (Lord of the Star of Long Life), he is the human manifestation of the star Canopus. In his left hand he carries a peach, a symbol of longevity.

would be sealed with a sticky, sweet substance to prevent him from delivering his report. Although the kitchen god became associated with the Daoist pantheon, he can just as easily be seen as part of family religious life. The same family might also have an altar to the Buddhist goddess of mercy.

Some Daoist deities were sponsored by the state. For example, the city god, Cheng Huang, was originally a protective god of city walls and moats, but his authority was extended to include the souls of the deceased. His role was altered by successive dynastic governments, which objectified him as a civil office – the office of Cheng Huang – which was in charge of dead souls in each locality. It became the custom for emperors to appoint deceased officials to the office of Cheng Huang for a term of three years. The official's rank in the "shadow" office was equivalent to the position he held when he was alive.

The Daoist pantheon includes not only heavenly beings but also historical figures who are honoured for their outstanding characteristics. Guan Yu, known for his loyalty and courage, was a general during the Three Kingdoms period (221–265CE); and the Tang emperor Ming Huang, who is patron deity of the theatre, kept a large company of dancers and musicians at court.

In modern times, many deities have been added to the Daoist pantheon, and the distinction between popular Buddhism and Daoism has become even more blurred. There is no equivalent in either tradition of lay membership, and anyone may go to pray or to burn incense in a Buddhist or Daoist temple. The same person may pray in the morning to the Buddhist goddess of mercy for the birth of a son, and, in the afternoon, to the Daoist god of medicine for the recovery of a sick relative.

In this 20th-century painting, the judge Guan Gong is shown presiding over the ninth court of hell, where the dead are either rewarded or given punishment. Shou Lao, the god of longevity, and other worthies are in attendance.

THE IMMORTALS

The Tianshan mountains in Xinjiang Province, whose ridges extend along the boundary between western China and the former Soviet Union, are believed to include the mythical Kunlunshan, home of Daoist immortals.

Ancient philosophical Daoism and religious Daoism differ sharply on the question of immortality. The philosopher Zhuang Zi (see pp.123–4) thought of death as a natural stage in existence and believed that even the practice of mourning the dead was misplaced. Daoist religious sects, on the other hand, shunned death and actively sought to achieve physical immortality. They were certain that life could at least be prolonged by one of the alchemical methods they were attempting to perfect (see pp.127, 129), and they were convinced that the secret of immortality was within their grasp.

Many Daoists were inspired by stories of such figures as Lao Zi (see pp.120, 127), who supposedly prolonged his life by nourishing his vital energy, and Lie Zi (see p.124), whose great spiritual power enabled him to ride on the wind. They also believed in immortals (*xian*), who were said to reside in a number of heavens. One of these heavens was Kunlun Mountain (Kunlunshan), in the far west of China. Kunlunshan was said to have nine upper levels reaching to heaven and nine lower levels reaching down to the abode of the dead. It was presided over by Xi Wang Mu, Queen Mother of the West, who in early myths appeared as an ogre, but in later stories became more gentle, even gracious.

Another immortal heaven, a group of magic islands, was mentioned in the *Book of Lie Zi* as well as in Sima Qian's *Historical Records*. Sima Qian wrote of three sacred mountains across the Eastern Sea where immortals and the elixir of life could be found. Many expeditions were sent to find these islands – including several that were commissioned by the First Qin Emperor, who unified China in 221BCE, and by Emperor Wu Di of the Han Dynasty – but none was ever able to reach their shores.

Early depictions of *xian* show them to be winged or covered with feathers, and the eastern coastal region of China, which bordered the ocean in which the magic isles were situated, was said to be inhabited by feathered bird-like people. The link between immortals and birds seems natural, because both were able to wander freely about the universe. Human immortals often rode on cranes, which were believed to have perfected techniques for prolonging life (see p.128).

Over the centuries Daoist writers created a new mythology of immortals from accounts of real or imaginary people who had attained the status of *xian*. This process culminated in the legends of the Eight Immortals, who were first associated with each other in the 15th century, although some of their names were known much earlier.

The Eight Immortals achieved eternal life in different ways. The first, Li Xuan, or Iron Crutch, was taught the secret by the Queen Mother of the West. Because he had a club foot, the queen presented him with an iron crutch, from which he took his nickname. He, in turn, passed the secret on to Zhongli Quan, the second immortal, who became the messenger of heaven and is often represented in art holding a feather fan.

The most famous of the Eight Immortals is Lü Dongbin. At an inn one night, Lü met a man named Han Zhongli, who started to heat a pot of wine for him. Lü fell asleep and dreamed that he was promoted to high office and enjoyed good fortune for fifty years. But then his luck ran out: he was disgraced and his family ruined. When Lü woke up, he saw that Han Zhongli still had not finished heating the wine and that in fact only a few minutes had passed. As a result of this dream, he became convinced of the vanity of worldly ambition and followed Han Zhongli into the mountains to seek the *Dao*. There he eventually became an immortal. He is often depicted carrying a sword.

The fourth immortal, Han Xiang, was a disciple of Lü Dongbin. When Han was close to achieving immortality, Lü took him to heaven to the tree that bore the peaches of eternal life. Han started to climb the tree but slipped and fell to the earth, becoming an immortal just before he hit the ground. He is frequently shown carrying a bouquet of flowers.

Cao Guojun, the fifth immortal, was a relative of the emperor. Disillusioned by corruption at the court, he went into the mountains to seek the *Dao*. At one point in his journey, he came to a river. He had no money to cross, so he tried to impress the boatman by showing him his golden badge of office. The boatman said, "You seek the *Dao*, yet you try to pull rank with me?" Cao was ashamed and threw his badge into the river. The boatman turned out to be Lü Dongbin in disguise. He took Cao as his disciple and taught him the Way. Cao Guojun is depicted carrying his golden badge.

The sixth immortal, Zhang Guo, lived during the Tang Dynasty (618–907CE). A skilful necromancer, with the ability to communicate with the dead in order to predict the future, he also possessed the power to grant offspring to newly-wed or childless couples. He is often depicted riding on a white mule,

The Eight Immortals, central to Daoist mythology, are often shown in art. These 19th-century Chinese ceramic figures represent, from left: Zhang Guo, Li Xuan (Iron Crutch), He Xiangu, Han Xiang, Lan Caihe and Zhongli Quan.

This Chinese painting on silk shows the immortal Ma Gu creating an orchard from the sea. According to legend, Ma Gu lived in the 2nd century CE. Incredibly beautiful, she achieved immortality at the age of eighteen and cultivated the ability to make the sea shallow.

facing either its head or its tail. The mule could cover vast distances each day, and Old Man Zhang Guo, as he is often called, could simply fold it up and put it in a bag when he reached the end of a journey. He may be shown holding peaches of immortality and a bag containing his folded mule.

Lan Caihe, the seventh immortal, was either a woman or a man "who didn't know how to be a man". One day, when she was collecting medicinal herbs in the mountains, she came across a beggar dressed in filthy rags, whose body was covered in sores. She washed and dressed his wounds. The beggar was in fact Li Xuan (Iron Crutch) in disguise, and he rewarded her kindness to him with the gift of eternal youth. Now an immortal, she toured the

country as a minstrel clad in a tattered blue gown, urging people to seek the *Dao*. She is often depicted holding a basket of fruit.

He Xiangu, the only immortal who was definitely female, acquired her immortality when a spirit told her to grind up and eat a "mother-of-pearl" stone, which could be found on a mountain near her home. She is shown as a maiden holding either a peach or a lotus blossom.

The Eight Immortals are often seen together in paintings and on porcelain, not travelling on clouds, which was their usual method of transport, but sailing across the Eastern Sea toward the Magic Islands.

These 19th-century Chinese ceramic figures represent He Xiangu (left), the only female of the Eight Immortals, and Lü Dongbin (right).

DAOIST SECTS

Daoism is far from a monolithic religion. The Daoist centres in China are largely autonomous but are bound together by basic doctrine. Early in its history, Daoism developed in three different areas and at three slightly different times, resulting in three traditions. The first branch evolved from the Five Bushels of Rice Society (see pp.132–3) in west and northwest China, and came to be known as the Heavenly Master tradition. The second, the Ling Bao tradition, emerged in southeast China and was derived from the Yellow Turban rebellion (see p.132). The third developed somewhat later on Mount Mao (Maoshan), near Nanjing, and was known as the Shang Qing tradition. This school's inspiration was said to have come from a woman named Wei Huacun, who fled the barbarian invasions in the north c.300CE. The Shang Qing apparently concentrated on meditation, while the two other traditions were orientated more toward ritual, but all three had features in common and could not strictly be considered separate sects. They shared a list of spirits' names, which also contained information about their jurisdictions, and a great many ritual texts setting out the means of attaining unity with the *Dao*.

In more recent times, there have been four major orders of orthodox Daoists in China. The Shang Qing order is still based on Mount Mao, and the Heavenly Master order is now centred on Mount Longhu in Jiangxi Province, southeast China. The two other orders are on Wudang Mountain in Hubei Province, central China, and Mount Hua in Shaanxi Province, northwest China. In addition, because of the remoteness of many Daoist centres and the organization of temples along master–apprentice lines (see p.134), many separate sects have sprung up, based on the teachings of local masters. These may number as many as seventy or eighty. Generally speaking, they can be divided into those that follow the Heavenly Master tradition, with its emphasis on ritual, and those that stress meditation.

REDHEADS AND BLACKHEADS

In Taiwan, where Daoism thrives today, Daoists are classified as blackheads and redheads. The normal Daoist headdress is black, but redhead Daoists wrap a red cloth around their heads when conducting ceremonies. Blackhead Daoists are orthodox, meaning that their ritual is based on canonical scripture and directed toward seeking unity with the *Dao*. They receive their certificates of ordination from the Heavenly Master (see p.133). This empowers them to minister to the souls of the dead, as well as to the living. Redhead Daoists are regarded as unorthodox and may only minister to the living. Because they are less restricted by tradition, their ceremonies are often more elaborate and spectacular than orthodox rituals. They also allow spectators to witness their ceremonies, whereas most orthodox priests do not. Although redhead Daoists are not unique to Taiwan, the country has now become their strongest base.

In Taiwan a redhead Daoist priest accompanies an open-air ceremony with a gong.

SHINTO

Shinto, the "Way of the *Kami* [Gods]", is the indigenous religion of Japan. Although stripped of the privileged status it enjoyed from 1868 until the end of the Second World War in 1945, and overshadowed in many respects by Buddhism, with which it has coexisted for 1500 years, the *kami* faith still permeates almost every aspect of Japanese life. Such ubiquitous customs as the daily bath and removing one's shoes before entering a home have roots in Shinto's pervasive concern with purification, and the reverence shown by the Japanese toward nature stems from the Shinto belief that spirit-beings occupy and govern the natural world.

Unlike Buddhism or Christianity, Shinto has no known founder. Its roots lie deep in Japanese prehistory; in a sense they extend into the land itself. The Jomon culture (*c.*9000–300BCE), the oldest Japanese prehistoric culture, venerated female figurines with exaggerated breasts and buttocks, but whether this is directly ancestral to Shinto is uncertain. However, the Yayoi culture (*c.*300BCE–300CE) presents features that are reminiscent of some of the central aspects of the *kami* faith. For example, small ceramic images of sacred storehouses dating from this period closely resemble the shrines dedicated to the rice and sun goddesses at Ise (see p.155), which, although periodically rebuilt, are the oldest manifestations of Shinto architecture.

A mikoshi *(portable shrine) is carried through the grounds of the Asakusa temple and shrine in Tokyo, during the annual Sanja festival. The Shinto shrine, which is adjacent to the Buddhist temple, is dedicated to three deified humans: two brothers, who retrieved the image of the Buddha from the Sumida River, and their master, who enshrined it.*

Archaic Shinto seems to have evolved by the beginning of the final phase of Japanese prehistory, the Kofun, or "Tumulus", era (*c.*300–550CE). Closely tied to the ancient clans, this belief system was intensely local, focusing on the spiritual power inherent in nearby topographical features and on the divine ancestors of particular clans and lineages. As the Yamato (Sun) clan gained influence over the others, its divine ancestor, the sun goddess, Amaterasu, rose to prominence accordingly. This laid the foundations for the emperor cult, which was relegated to a symbolic role during the long reign of the shoguns (12th–19th centuries), but returned to dominate Shinto in modern times.

In 1868, after more than 250 years of rule by the Tokugawa Shogunate, the Meiji Restoration returned power to the emperor, and in 1871 Shinto was established as the state religion. Along with the newly instituted imperial army and navy, "State Shinto" became a principal mechanism for fostering Japanese nationalism and loyalty to the emperor. During this phase all Shinto priests became government employees, and the beliefs and practices that they promoted were overseen by the Bureau of Shrines in Tokyo. The word "Shinto" dates from this period; before then the religion was simply the worship of the *kami*.

State Shinto came to an abrupt end with the conclusion of the Second World War in 1945. The emperor renounced all claims to divinity, and Japan's post-war constitution of 1947 specifically prohibited the state from having any involvement in religious affairs. As a result of these changes, Shinto quickly reverted to what it had been for most of its long history: a loosely organized collection of shrines (*jinja*) dedicated to an almost infinite number of *kami*. Although there is a pantheon of gods and goddesses, such as Amaterasu, who are worshipped throughout Japan, the *kami* are for the most part unique to their communities. Indeed, the primary feature of contemporary Shinto is its localism. Each

Sumo wrestling, the Japanese national sport, derives from an ancient Shinto ritual honouring the kami. *The canopy over the* dohyo *(ring) is reminiscent of a Shinto shrine, the referee wears a costume similar to that worn by a Shinto priest and the extensive throwing of salt (thought to have magical properties) before a match is believed to purify the ring.*

shrine, from the sacred Ise complex to the most obscure country *jinja*, is self-governing and has at least one or two distinctive rituals and customs, the most visible being the annual festival, in which young men and women carry a portable shrine on their shoulders through the streets of a village or neighbourhood. Despite the shadow of Japanese militarism and imperialism that fell across Shinto in the early post-war period, the religion continues to thrive and to command the affection, if not absolute loyalty, of the majority of the Japanese people.

SACRED AND MYTHOLOGICAL JAPAN

Japan's landscape is crowded with sacred places, which are believed to be favoured by the gods. The Yamato region, the heartland of ancient Japan, is particularly sacred, because it was here that the legendary first emperor, Jimmu-tenno, a descendant of the sun goddess, Amaterasu, established his court, after a march of conquest that began in northern Kyushu.

KEY

Yamato region (corresponds roughly to present-day Nara Prefecture)

● Modern cities

• Sacred sites

· Mythological sites

▲ Sacred mountains

HOKKAIDO

Sapporo

Akita

Sendai

SEA OF JAPAN

JAPAN

Nikko

HONSHU

Tokyo

Fuji-san

Izumo-taisha

Hi River

Kyoto (Heian)

Osaka

Nara

Tenri

Nagoya

Ise-jingu

Onogoro

Ama-no-Iwato

PACIFIC OCEAN

Hiroshima

Miyajima

Nachi

SHIKOKU

Nagasaki

KYUSHU

Takachio-san

THE PRINCIPAL *KAMI*

Shinto belief and practice revolve around the worship of *kami*, divinities who oversee almost every aspect of nature and human life. The ancient Japanese texts assert that there are an infinite number of *kami*, from the spirits who animate features of the environment to immediate family ancestors to actual gods and goddesses. Many *kami* live in the sky and come down to earth periodically to visit sacred places and shrines. They are considered so sacred that worshippers must purify themselves before entering shrine precincts or participating in festivals (see p.157), which are held in their honour.

The most important Shinto divinity is the sun goddess, Amaterasu (the "Person Who Makes the Heavens Shine"), who is both chief of the pantheon and divine ancestor of the imperial family. She is worshipped at the Ise-*jingu* (see p.155), which is the most sacred shrine in Japan.

According to the *Kojiki* (712CE) and the *Nihonshoki* (720CE), the primary sources of Japanese myth, Amaterasu is the daughter of the heavenly divinity Izanagi-no-mikoto (the "August Male"), who is sometimes referred to as the Japanese Adam. Izanagi descended from heaven to the island of Onogoro (see map, p.147), and began procreating with his wife and sister, Izanami-no-mikoto (the "August Female"). The couple produced the islands that comprise the Japanese archipelago and then gave birth to a series of gods and goddesses. However, Izanami died from burns that she received while giving birth to the fire god.

A statue of Daikokuten, one of the "Seven Lucky Gods", from the Narita-san temple in Kuruma. Daikokuten represents prosperity and well-being and is a tutelary god of the kitchen, favoured by cooks and restaurants.

Frightened by Susano, Amaterasu withdrew into a cave known as Ama-no-Iwato *(see map, p.147), plunging the world into darkness. She had to be tricked into returning, as shown in this 19th-century print triptych.*

TENJIN: PORTRAIT OF A *KAMI*

The popular *kami* Tenjin is the spirit of the 9th-century scholar Sugawara Michizane. After achieving an outstanding reputation, Michizane fell victim to political intrigue and was forced into exile on the island of Kyushu, where he eventually died an unhappy death. Shortly afterward, a series of disasters struck Heian, the imperial capital (modern Kyoto). These were thought to be the result of Michizane's angry spirit seeking vengeance. To placate the ghost, the court enshrined the dead scholar as a *kami* under the name Tenjin (literally, "Heaven Person"). The magnificent Kitano Shrine in Kyoto was built in his honour, and the new god soon became established as the patron of learning and scholarship. His cult

A detail from a 13th-century scroll shows the banishment of Michizane (later deified as Tenjin).

spread throughout Japan, and students (and their parents) regularly visit Tenjin shrines to ask the *kami* for his assistance in passing exams.

After an unsuccessful attempt to bring his beloved back from the Land of the Dead, Izanagi purified himself by bathing in a sacred river. Amaterasu was born from his left eye when he wiped the water from it. Tsukiyomi, the moon god, was born from his right eye, and Susano, the god of storms (also known as the "Raging Male"), emerged from his nose. Izanagi awarded sovereignty over heaven and earth to Amaterasu. However, Susano, who had been given dominion of the sea, was unhappy with his lot and challenged his sister's authority. After a dramatic confrontation, in the course of which Amaterasu withdrew into a cave, Susano was banished from heaven. He descended to earth, landing in Izumo near the headwaters of the Hi River (see map, p.147).

Eventually, Amaterasu sent her grandson Honinigi to the mortal world bearing three talismans of sovereignty – a sacred mirror, a magical sword and a wondrous fertility jewel called a *magatama*. According to tradition, he landed at Mount Takachio, in Kyushu (see map, p.147), and struck a

deal with Susano's descendant Okuninushi, the "Great Lord of the Country" (also known as Daikoku-sama). In return for the latter's loyalty, Amaterasu recognized Okuninushi as the perpetual protector of the imperial family, which was later founded by Honinigi's great-grandson, Jimmu-tenno. Okuninushi is enshrined at Izumo-*taisha* (see map, p.147), which, after Ise, is the most important Shinto shrine in Japan.

Other prominent *kami* include Hachiman, the spirit of the semi-legendary warrior Emperor Ojin and the closest Shinto comes to a god of war, and the "Seven Lucky Gods" (*Shichifukujin*), each of whom personifies a desirable characteristic or condition. The most popular of the Lucky Gods are Daikokuten, who is typically depicted with a large sack slung over his left shoulder, and Ebisu, who carries a fishing-rod in his right hand and a sea bream under his left arm. Sometimes said to be father and son, Daikokuten and Ebisu both personify wealth and material abundance. The others in this group include Benten (skill in music and the arts), Fukurokuju (popularity), Hotei (contentment and magnanimity), Jurojin (longevity) and Bishamonten (benevolent authority).

New additions are frequently made to the roster of major *kami*. For example, the spirit of Emperor Meiji (1868–1912), during whose reign Japan moved from being a backward East Asian country to the status of a world power, is venerated in the largest shrine in Tokyo, the Meiji-*jingu*; and the spirit of Ieyasu, the first Tokugawa shogun (1543–1616), is magnificently enshrined at Nikko (see map, p.147). This ability to grow and change with the times is part of the essential genius of Shinto.

SHINTO DEMONS AND THE QUESTION OF EVIL

Not all *kami* are beneficent. Shinto also recognizes numerous demons (*oni*), who are responsible for a wide variety of mortal troubles. Most *oni* are invisible, but some are animal spirits who have the ability to possess humans and must be exorcised by a priest. Fox spirits are considered to be especially dangerous.

Unlike Western religions – and even some Buddhist sects – Shinto does not believe that there is an absolute dichotomy of good and evil. Rather, all phenomena, both animate and inanimate, are thought to possess both "rough" and "gentle" characteristics, and it is possible for a given entity to manifest either of these characteristics depending on the circumstances. Thus, in spite of their malevolence, *oni* are somewhat ambivalent characters. For example, the malicious fox spirit is also closely associated with Inari, the rice god, who is an extremely popular and charitable *kami*. Inari is believed to control the quality of the rice harvest and is also worshipped as the patron of general prosperity. Statues of his messenger, the fox, flank his image at Inari shrines. Another example of this ambivalence is Susano (see p.149), who, after his banishment from heaven, became a positive figure, slaying a dragon and saving a maiden in distress. In all cases, the misfortunes inflicted by *oni* are seen as the result of a temporary disruption of the natural order of things, and not the manifestation of an inherent evil force.

Oni *(demons) exist both on earth and in a subterranean hell called Jigoku, depicted in this 19th-century Japanese painting. Some* oni *have both positive and negative aspects, depending on the context. For example, the ugly demon Tengu (see left) can also be the benevolent guardian of* kami, *and for this reason he is often impersonated at Shinto festivals.*

SHRINES AND SACRED PLACES

Shinto has always been a highly personal and local religion, except during the period in which it became established as the state cult (1871–1945; see p.146). Its shrines (*jinja*), which are dedicated to the various gods (*kami*; see pp.148–50), are scattered throughout Japan. Because *kami* are believed to animate features of the environment, many natural places are also considered sacred in the Shinto faith (see map, p.147). Fuji-*san*, Japan's most sacred mountain, is considered to be a *kami*, and people who climb it are in effect performing an act of worship. The same is true for those who visit the great Nachi Waterfall in Wakayama Prefecture, also believed to be a powerful *kami*.

The Shinto shrine serves as the focus of a great many rituals and associated activities (see pp.157–8). A mother may visit a shrine to petition the local god to help her child pass a difficult university entrance examination, or an elderly gentleman might ask the same *kami* to find his granddaughter a suitable husband. Such personal requests comprise the most ubiquitous form of religious observance in Shinto, but the most important is the annual or biannual festival (*matsuri*; see pp.157, 159), in which the local *kami* is fêted by the community.

Because Shinto is such an ancient tradition, its shrines reflect the evolution of Japanese history and technology. The earliest *jinja* were simple outdoor altars, often carved from local rock, upon which offerings could be laid. As time went on, these altars were enclosed and the new structures came to resemble the ceramic storehouses of the Yayoi culture (see

This sacred tree is adorned with gohei, *white paper streamers that indicate the presence of gods.*

p.144). The most sacred Shinto shrine, the Ise-*jingu* (see p.155), which holds the imperial sacred mirror (see p.149), is an example of this early phase in Shinto architecture.

Shinto underwent a transformation when Buddhism was introduced into Japan around the end of the 6th century CE (see pp.160–61). Not only did the theology of Shinto adapt to the alien faith, but also its shrines began to be built in a distinctive Chinese style, with bright colours and elaborate ornamentation, marking a significant departure from the simplicity of Ise.

Modern Shinto shrines are built in diverse styles and sizes, ranging from tiny *jinja* on the rooftops of highrise buildings to vast complexes, such as the Meiji-*jingu* in Tokyo and the Heian Shrine in Kyoto. However, most shrines have a fundamentally similar layout and are situated, whenever possible, amid trees and gardens, again reflecting the importance of nature in Shinto belief.

To enter the precinct of a shrine, a worshipper must first pass under the *torii* (gate), which represents the threshold separating the outer, secular world from the sacred world of the gods. It will usually be festooned with *gohei*, torn strips of paper arranged in pairs, which symbolize the presence of *kami*. Inside the precinct there will be a stone trough containing pure water and at least one bamboo dipper. The worshipper scoops out some water, pours it over (*text continues on page 154*)

OVERLEAF *The island of Miyajima ("Shrine Island"; see map, p.147) was considered so sacred that people had to approach it by boat through the famous giant* torii *(gate).*

Wooden good-luck charms at a shrine in Kyoto have been left by worshippers for the attention of the local gods.

his or her hands, and lightly rinses the mouth, thereby purifying the body both inside and out, and making it fit to enter the presence of the gods.

The shrine itself is typically composed of two principal elements: the *honden* (sanctuary), which holds the image of the *kami* and is rarely, if ever, visited by laypeople, and the *haiden* (oratory). The worshipper approaches the *haiden*, makes a small monetary offering, and either rings a bell attached to a long rope or claps twice to attract the attention of the *kami*. Then he or she bows, pressing the hands together in an attitude of prayer, and silently asks a favour of the *kami*. When the request has been made, the worshipper claps to signal the end of the prayer. If the favour is granted, the petitioner is expected to return to the shrine to thank the *kami*.

Larger shrines typically have a public meeting hall, a stage for ritual performances, one or more storehouses, in which portable shrines (*mikoshi*) are kept between festivals, and stalls where "altar girls" (*miko*; see p.158) sell good-luck charms and personal fortunes. If the buyer approves of the fortune, he or she will tie it to a tree in the grounds of the shrine so that the local god may take note of it.

Today all Shinto shrines are managed by groups of laypeople who pay the head priest (*guji*), as well as the other priests (*kannushi*), and generally oversee the affairs of the shrine. Some major shrines, such as Tokyo's Meiji-*jingu*, have dozens of priests, whereas small neighbourhood *jinja* often have no

The Kasuga shrine in Nara, with its vermilion paint and upturned Chinese-style roof, is an example of the influence of Chinese civilization on shrine architecture in Japan.

full-time *guji* and must retain the services of a priest from another, larger (and wealthier) shrine to perform important ceremonies.

In the home every traditional Japanese family has a miniature shrine, or *kamidana* (literally, a "god-shelf"). This contains a small replica of a *honden* (sanctuary) with the names of family ancestors who are honoured as *kami*. An elderly member of the household, often the grandmother, tends the *kamidana* by placing on it each morning small cups of saké and dishes containing a few grains of rice and vegetables. At shrines priests distribute similar offerings, because all *kami* must periodically be nourished if they are to perform at peak efficiency.

THE ISE-*JINGU*

The most sacred of all Shinto shrine complexes, the Grand Shrines at Ise (Ise-*jingu*; see map, p.147) are dedicated to two major divinities: the rice goddess, enshrined in the "Outer Shrine" (*Geku*), and the sun goddess, Amaterasu, celebrated in the "Inner Shrine" (*Naiku*). The latter holds the sacred mirror, one of the prime symbols of the sun goddess, which was supposedly brought to earth by Amaterasu's grandson,

Honinigi (see p.149). The emperor traditionally makes an annual pilgrimage to the *Naiku* to report the year's events to his divine ancestor as well as to pray for a good year's rice crop.

The Ise-*jingu* is distinguished from other Shinto shrines by the fact that it is torn down and rebuilt every twenty years (the most recent rebuilding occurred in 1993). This custom, which began in the 8th century CE, serves by extension to

renew the enshrined divinities. The new shrine buildings, which are located on carefully maintained sites immediately adjacent to the previous ones, are identical to the ones they replace; the carpenters responsible for the rebuilding typically come from families who have participated in this activity for generations. Thus, the Ise shrines are steeped in ancient tradition, but at the same time always appear new and fresh.

*This 18th-century woodblock print depicts worshippers visiting the Ise-*jingu, *the most sacred shrine in Japan.*

RITUAL AND CEREMONY

Shinto worship is for the most part a highly personal affair, distinguishing the religion from such Western traditions as Christianity and Judaism, which emphasize communal rituals. Individuals will visit a shrine when they have a particular request to make of the *kami*, to thank the deity for a favour previously granted or to mark a special occasion. However, the annual or biannual *matsuri* (shrine festival; see p.159) is an outstanding exception.

A wedding couple in formal dress. Most Japanese marriage ceremonies are still based on Shinto rites.

worshippers during this period that the trains are packed and the crowds are regulated by the police. Long lines of worshippers throw coins in the offering box and then purchase sacred arrows, symbolic of good fortune for the coming year. In some neighbourhoods, individuals and families who are formally connected to a particular shrine annually dispose of their old miniature shrines by removing them from the god-shelf in their home (see p.155) and placing them in a large pile or pit near the *jinja*. These shrines are then ritually burned by the priests. Their replacements, purchased from a shrine shop before the old year ends, symbolize spiritual renewal.

As much an expression of neighbourhood or community solidarity as it is a religious ritual, the *matsuri* is by far the most important event that occurs at a Shinto shrine. The central feature of such a festival is the sacred procession in which a portable shrine (*mikoshi*) bearing an image of the local god is carried through the streets, often by saké-fortified youths, in order to honour and entertain the *kami*. The *mikoshi* is shaken about as much as possible, because this is believed to enhance the *kami*'s enjoyment. The activity serves to reinforce the common identity of the shrine's "parishioners". It is also considered a means of purifying and making sacred all of those who carry the *mikoshi*, as well as the community through which it is carried.

The yearly cycle, especially the coming of the New Year, is also extremely significant. Most Japanese people visit Shinto shrines during the three-day *shogatsu-matsuri* (New Year's festival: 1–3 January). Indeed, major shrines such as Tokyo's Meiji-*jingu* or the Heian Shrine in Kyoto attract so many

The rice cycle, from springtime planting to the summer harvest, is another seasonal activity that is full of Shinto symbolism and ritual. The rice goddess is implored to visit the fields and make them abundant. Such ritual is naturally more important in rural areas, but the whole country celebrates the emperor's annual planting of the first rice plants in a special paddy at the Imperial Palace in Tokyo.

In keeping with Shinto's emphasis on this world, nature, fertility and renewal, the majority of Japanese marriages are solemnized by *kannushi* (Shinto priests) rather than by Buddhist priests, although few actually take place at shrines. Most major hotels and "wedding palaces" appoint Shinto priests to perform the ceremony, which involves mutual sipping of saké and the recitation of prayers. Conversely, only a very small number of funerals – mostly those of *kannushi* and of members of the imperial family – are performed according to Shinto rites. The vast majority of Japanese funerals are

Worshippers parade with a mikoshi *(portable shrine) in front of the spectacular waterfall in Akita, northwestern Honshu, which is thought to be favoured by the local* kami.

conducted by Buddhist priests, as Buddhism is believed to carry the soul into the next life (see pp.72–3).

Shinto worshippers always purify themselves before entering a shrine precinct (see pp.151, 154). However, on special occasions, such as the first visit to a shrine after the birth of a child, they may also see a priest for *oharai* (ritual purification). This is the most common ritual performed at a Shinto *jinja* and involves the priest waving a sacred *sakaki* branch

*A Shinto priest (*kannushi*) carries a sacred* sakaki *branch. Sakaki, which means "prosperity tree", is used in ritual purification ceremonies.*

over the petitioner's head. Worshippers believe that *oharai* removes accumulated pollution and restores

internal bodily equilibrium as well as the individual's harmonious relationship with the outer world.

Oharai is not enacted only for people, nor is it restricted to the shrine. Before construction begins on a Japanese building, a Shinto priest is usually employed to purge the new site of any evil spirits that might be present. Many Japanese people believe that a site will be unlucky unless this ritual purification is performed. People might also ask a priest to perform *oharai* over a new car, believing that this will ensure its safety on the road.

MIKO

In ancient times, and to this day in some regions of rural Japan, *miko* (shrine virgins) were regarded as true shamans who were able to be possessed by the *kami* and deliver their messages. This heritage is reflected in the ritual dances that are sometimes performed by *miko* during ceremonies: their swaying motions are said to derive from what was once an ecstatic or trance state. Today, the primary duties of these "altar girls", who are readily identifiable by their white upper garments and red skirts, are to sell fortunes and good-luck charms and to assist the priests in a variety of rituals. Most are teenagers, because once married they can no longer serve in this capacity. For a girl to work as a *miko* brings honour to her family, and often several generations of women in the same household serve as *miko* at the local shrine. Large shrines such as the Meiji-*jingu* have numerous *miko* from all parts of Tokyo.

A miko *performs a* kagura *dance, which is a celebration of the renewal of life.*

A NEIGHBOURHOOD *MATSURI*

The following account of a Shinto festival (*matsuri*) is based on the author's research in "Daigaku-cho", a Tokyo neighbourhood whose *matsuri* is typical of countless other festivals throughout Japan, although the *kami* that is honoured may of course be different.

Each year, on the first weekend of September, the Tenso-*jinja*, as the local shrine is called, jointly sponsors a *matsuri* with Daigaku-cho's neighbourhood association (*cho-kai*). Every third year the festival becomes a *taisai* ("major celebration"), which means that a *shin ko sai* (literally, "god go around") will be held. In ordinary years the portable shrine (*mikoshi*) that is carried through the streets belongs to the *cho-kai*, and the sacred image of the Tenso-*jinja*'s *kami* (Amaterasu; see pp.148–9) is not present. These interim festivals, as well as the events of the first day of a *taisai*, during which the *cho-kai*'s *mikoshi* is also carried, are referred to locally as "shadow *matsuri*".

The festival is transformed into a "major celebration" on the second day of a *taisai*, when the head priest (*guji*) of a larger, nearby shrine (like many neighbourhood shrines, the Tenso-*jinja* is too small to afford the services of a full-time *guji*) carefully removes the sacred image of Amaterasu from the sanctuary and places it inside the waiting *mikoshi*. After he chants an appropriate prayer, in this instance addressed to the sun goddess, and performs *oharai* (ritual purification; see p.158), approximately fifty men and women who live in the neighbourhood hoist the *mikoshi* to their shoulders and begin the

Neighbourhood girls carry a mikoshi *through the streets of "Daigaku-cho". Women started carrying portable Shinto shrines in many parts of Japan in the late 1970s.*

procession. Chanting "*Wa-shoi! Wa-shoi!*" (untranslatable) and moving in an undulating, bob-and-weave fashion, they make their way up one narrow street and down another, stopping frequently at predetermined locations for refreshments provided by the neighbourhood association. The procession includes the *guji*, who walks a few steps ahead of the *mikoshi*, the shrine's "deacons", a local high-school student beating a *taiko* drum, several costumed attendants and a young man wearing a Tengu mask, whose function is to ward off any malevolent spirits that might disrupt the proceedings (see p.150). The chief lay officer of the shrine also occupies a prominent place in the procession, as do his fellow "deacons", all of whom wear traditional Japanese clothing. The mood is joyous rather than solemn, and the presence of the *kami* often engenders a feeling of divinity among the participants.

The party finally returns to the *jinja* in the late afternoon. The priest removes the image of the *kami* from the *mikoshi* and places it back in the sanctuary, where it will remain for the next three years.

In the evening, neighbourhood families gather in the grounds of the shrine to eat food from stalls that have been set up by itinerant vendors, purchase souvenirs, and watch a *kagura* (sacred theatre) troop perform scenes from the mythological books the *Kojiki* and the *Nihonshoki*. In Daigaku-cho this widespread practice has recently been abandoned in favour of more popular, although still traditional, entertainment by a song-and-dance troop.

SHINTO AND BUDDHISM:
1500 YEARS OF COEXISTENCE

Buddhism has coexisted with Shinto in Japan since 593CE, when Prince Shotoku Taishi established it as the official religion of the imperial court. This long-term synchronism of two vastly different belief systems, one of which is indigenous and the other imported, is perhaps the most important single difference between Japan and the West when it comes to attitudes toward religion. In the West, when Christianity intruded into the Germanic and Celtic regions, the indigenous religions – which in many respects were quite similar to Shinto – were wiped out in the name of orthodoxy. "Pagan" temples and shrines to gods such as Odin, Thor and Lugh were torn down and churches and cathedrals were built in their place; indeed, this pattern has persisted into modern times as missionaries have carried Christianity to almost every corner of the planet.

In Japan the Buddhist missionaries took a different approach. Instead of tearing down the Shinto *jinja*, they built their temples nearby and proclaimed that the *kami* and the *bodhisattvas* (in Japanese, *bosatsu*) of Mahayana Buddhism (see pp.84–5) were the same thing. As this ideology crystallized, a form of Shinto developed known as Ryobo Shinto (Dual Aspect Shinto), in which *kami* and *bosatsu* were melded into single divine entities with alternative manifestations. This theology was favoured by the Tendai Buddhist sects (see p.87) and led, in some

TENRIKYO: A SHINTO SECT

By the end of the Meiji era in 1912, thirteen Shinto-based sects were recognized by the Japanese government. One of these was the Tenrikyo (Heavenly Truth) sect. It was founded in 1838 by a farmer's wife named Miki Nakayama (1798–1887), who lived near the ancient capital Nara (see map, p.147). One night, while caring for her sick son, she went into trance and was possessed by a *kami* who identified himself as Ten-taishogun, the "Great Heavenly Generalissimo". In a series of possessions, Ten-taishogun revealed that he and his nine

subordinate entities were the only true *kami*, and that they had chosen Nakayama to spread their message. This message was eventually set down in a 1711-verse poem called the *Ofudesaki* (literally, "The Tip of the Divine Writing Brush"). Completed in 1883, after fifteen years of work, the poem contains the revelations that Nakayama received concerning the nature of heaven, the *kami* who dwell there and the role of humankind in the divine scheme of things – a role which is analogous to that played by a child with regard to his or her parents.

In time, Tenrikyo developed into a major Shinto sect, with its headquarters in Tenri City, just south of Nara. Today it claims a membership of almost two million people, and is one of the most successful of Japan's "new religions".

Although its concern with the afterlife reflects some features of Pure Land Buddhist theology (see p.87), the core of Tenrikyo's doctrine stems directly from the fundamental Shinto concept of *kami*, and the idea that the universe and all that it contains is animated by a hierarchy of deities.

Like many Shinto divinities, the war god Hachiman, who is the spirit of the legendary emperor Ojin, has a Buddhist aspect. In this painting from the Kamakura period (1185–1333), he is depicted in Buddhist robes as either a bosatsu *(bodhisattva) or as a Buddhist priest.*

cases, to Buddhist management of Shinto shrines and combined priesthood. It also produced some remarkable visual art in the form of *mandalas* depicting the *kami* as ordinary humans and the *bodhisattvas* as more ethereal beings drifting in clouds of smoke above the Shinto deities' heads (a good example is the famous Kasuga *Mandala*).

Even where Shinto managed to resist the penetration of specific Buddhist beliefs – the best example is the Ise-*jingu*, from which Buddhist priests were barred until modern times – many Buddhist deities were adopted as *kami*. Two of the Seven Lucky Gods (see pp.149–50), Benten and Bishamonten, are clear examples of this practice. A third, Daikokuten, is what the Shinto scholar Genichi Kato (1873–1965) calls a "dual god" – that is, although Daikokuten was

originally a Buddhist deity, the fact that his name sounds like Daikoku-sama (also known as Okuninushi; see p.149) has caused him to be identified with this indigenous Shinto *kami* and venerated alongside him at Izumo-*taisha*. Moreover, most major Buddhist temple complexes include at least one associated Shinto shrine.

The complementary aspects of the two faiths are perhaps most apparent in the religious attitudes of the Japanese people themselves. Except for adherents of some of the "new religions", such as Tenrikyo (see left), most Japanese readily admit to being both Shintoists and Buddhists and see no contradiction in this whatsoever. For example, the great majority of Japanese people are married according to Shinto rites and buried according to Buddhist ones, emphasizing the commonly held perception that Shinto is the "life religion" while Buddhism is the "death religion". People visit Buddhist temples during their lifetimes for many of the same reasons that they visit Shinto shrines (see pp.157–8), but still most Japanese cemeteries are attached to Buddhist temples rather than to Shinto *jinja*.

Buddhism is not the only foreign belief system to have influenced Shinto. Although ancestor worship almost certainly existed in Japan before the impact of Chinese culture in the 6th century, Confucianism, which was introduced into the country by the same missionaries who introduced Buddhism, certainly gave it a strong impetus (see p.107). Moreover, two of the Seven Lucky Gods, Hotei and Fukurokuju (see p.150), are Daoist in origin. Like all religions, Shinto has drawn extensively on the belief systems with which it has come into contact. Despite these foreign influences, however, the core of the *kami* faith remains essentially intact. From all indications it continues to play the primary role in the spiritual life of the vast majority of contemporary Japanese people, no matter what other religious or philosophical ideas they may also espouse.

GLOSSARY

Words in SMALL CAPITAL LETTERS within an entry are cross-referred.

HINDUISM

adharma evil; disorder; immorality; unrighteousness; compare DHARMA

ahimsa not killing; non-violence

Arjuna hero of the *BHAGAVAD GITA*, one of the five Pandava brothers

artha wealth, success; one of the four aims of human life (PURUSARTHAS)

ashrama a stage of life in the Hindu life-cycle; also, a forest hermitage or retreat

atman the individual self or soul

avatar the descent of a god in bodily form

bali a restless spirit

Bhagavad Gita the Song of the Lord, a section of the *MAHABHARATA* in which KRISHNA advises ARJUNA to fulfil his duty regardless of the results of his actions

bhakti-marga the path of devotion, in which spiritual liberation (MOKSHA) is achieved by surrendering all one's works and desires to god

Brahma the creator god

brahmacarin studentship; the first of the four stages of life

brahman the impersonal absolute; the universal soul which is present in all things

brahmin the highest of the four classes; the priestly class (also written as *brahmana*)

darshana the experience of seeing the deity

deva a god; a generic name for gods used in the Vedas and later texts; see also under Buddhism glossary

devi a goddess; feminine form of DEVA

dharma responsibility; ethics; law; moral and cosmic order. The principle of order that governs both the universe and individual lives; see also under Buddhism glossary

Divali Hindu Festival of Lights

Durga aggressive goddess who was created from the energy of the gods in order to defeat the demon Mahisa

Ganesha elephant-headed deity, son of PARVATI and SHIVA; Remover of Obstacles

Hanuman the monkey god; warrior and devotee of RAMA who rescues SITA from the demon Ravana

japa repetition of the divine names of god; a popular devotional meditation

jnana-marga the path of knowledge, characterized by study, meditation and asceticism, leading to spiritual liberation (MOKSHA)

Kali the "black one", the name of one of the terrifying aspects of the Goddess

kama love; pleasure; one of the four aims of human life (PURUSARTHAS)

karma ritual act; work; action; the law of karma refers to how the results of an individual's actions affect his or her future rebirth; see also under Buddhism glossary

karma-marga path of action, leading to spiritual liberation (MOKSHA)

Krishna the eighth AVATAR of VISHNU; this dark-blue god figures prominently in the *Bhagavata Purana*, as a hero and lover, and in the *BHAGAVAD GITA*, as the adviser and charioteer of ARJUNA

kshatriya the warrior and kingly class

Lakshmi goddess of prosperity and good fortune; consort of VISHNU

linga phallic symbol of SHIVA

Mahabharata great martial epic of the Hindus which, in its telling of the great war between the Pandavas and the Kauravas, provides guidance on moral living and the pursuit of MOKSHA

mantra a word or verbal formula that is recited, often as an aid to meditation

moksha release or liberation; release from ignorance and the cycle of rebirths, often characterized as the union of an individual (ATMAN) with the divine (BRAHMAN)

Parvati daughter of the Himalayas; consort of SHIVA

pradakshina ritual of circumambulation

pralaya the ocean of dissolution which follows the destruction of the universe and precedes its re-creation

prasada grace; the grace of god; also the food presented to the deity at a temple and then returned to the devotee as a sign of god's favour

puja ceremony of worshipping a deity

Puranas sacred collection of legends and ritual practice

purusarthas the four aims of human life, namely, DHARMA, ARTHA, KAMA and MOKSHA

purusha the cosmic man, from whose dismembered parts, in certain Hindu myths, the world evolved

Rama hero of the *RAMAYANA* and avatar of VISHNU

Ramayana a great Hindu epic, which tells of RAMA's defeat of the demon Ravana and the rescuing of his wife SITA

sanatana dharma the eternal and divine order of the universe

samsara the material world; the process of rebirth into the material world; see also under Buddhism glossary

samskara ceremonies that mark different developmental stages in a Hindu's life

sannyasin a renunciant; one who has entered the fourth stage of life

Sarasvati goddess of wisdom and learning; consort of BRAHMA

shakti divine energy, characterized as feminine and personified by the Goddess

Shiva the erotic ascetic, whose divine energy, represented by his ever-erect phallus, has the potential to destroy as well as renew creation

shruti (hearing) refers to the sacred Hindu texts that are transmitted orally – namely, the Vedas; *shruti* are believed to be of divine origin

shudra the class of labourers

Sita heroine of the *RAMAYANA* held up as the ideal Hindu wife and woman

smriti   remembering; refers to those authoritative religious texts which are popularly preserved in the Hindu memory; they are composed by humans, although divinely inspired

svadharma   an individual's DHARMA, as determined by his or her age, class and gender

tirtha   ford or crossing; a term used to refer to a site of intensified sacredness, wherein the divine intersects with the mundane world

upanayana   "sacred thread" ceremony that initiates a boy from the three upper classes into a period of Vedic study in preparation for him assuming the moral and ritual responsibilities of a mature Hindu

Upanishads   mystical texts of speculative philosophy

vaishya   the farmer and merchant class

vanaprastha   forest-dweller; the third of the four stages of human life in the ideal ASHRAMA system

Veda   knowledge; specifically the sacred knowledge revealed in the Vedas

Vishnu   the sustainer and protector of the universe; his avatars descend from time to time to re-establish order in the world of humans

vivaha   the wedding ceremony that initiates a couple into the householder stage of life

Yama   god of death; also known as Dharma-raja, king of DHARMA

yoga   discipline; a classical system of Hindu philosophy teaching a practical means of enlightenment

yuga   an era of the world

BUDDHISM

Most of the key terms in this chapter are written in Sanskrit, a classical Indian language in which many important Buddhist texts have been preserved, and in which Buddhist terms are most familiar to the Western reader.

anatman   (no-self) one of the three marks of all conditioned existence, which states that nothing (including persons) has an inherent enduring essence

anitya   one of the three marks of all conditioned existence, according to which all things are impermanent

arhat   a "worthy one", a fully enlightened being that has cut the bonds of SAMSARA, and will never be reborn again

bodhisattva   a being intent on enlightenment. The *bodhisattva* strives to become a fully enlightened BUDDHA and has come to epitomize the ideal of the Buddhist path according to the MAHAYANA tradition

Buddha   a fully awakened being who realizes enlightenment by his own means. There have been many Buddhas – the last of which was SIDDHARTHA GAUTAMA, the Sage of the Shakyas (Shakyamuni) – and there will be many more Buddhas to come.

dana   Buddhist virtue of giving and actively practising charity; the first of the six perfections

deva   the divine beings ("gods") that inhabit certain celestial realms; see also under Hinduism glossary

dharma   in Buddhism, the Truth, the Law and the teaching of the BUDDHA, which is reality itself; see also under Hinduism glossary

dhyana   mental absorption; the kind of trance obtained through the practice of SHAMATHA meditation

duhkha   literally, "suffering"; designates the antithesis of liberation and enlightenment

Four Noble Truths   (*aryasatya*) one of the typical expositions of the content of the BUDDHA's enlightenment and of the whole teaching of Buddhism itself

karma   the law of moral retribution according to which every deed or moral act has its consequential results; see also under Hinduism glossary

karuna   compassion, or the moral sentiment of caring for others and striving to assist them in obtaining enlightenment; along with PRAJNA (wisdom), one of the key constituents of Buddhist practice

Mahayana   The Great Vehicle, an influential minority movement in Buddhist India that gained prominence as it expanded to north and east Asia. Mahayana lays emphasis on the path of the BODHISATTVA

mandala   a cosmogram, a meditational device that is a representation of the Buddhist universe

Nikaya   the five principle "collections" of the discourses of the BUDDHA in the PALI CANON

nirvana   the liberation ensuing from the eradication of greed, hatred and delusion, which tie beings to SAMSARA

Pali Canon   the oldest surviving recension of the Buddhist canon extant in an Indian language and the canon used by THERAVADA Buddhists

parinirvana   the BUDDHA's final and complete extinction, associated with the death of his earthly body

prajna   wisdom; a direct realization of things as they really are, which is tantamount to enlightenment in Buddhism

samadhi   (concentration) the cultivation and practice of mental abilities, predominantly through meditative concentration

samsara   the endless cycle of birth and rebirth in which beings experience DUHKHA and from which they strive to gain liberation; see also under Hinduism glossary

Sangha   the Buddhist community of enlightened beings and the worldly community of monks and nuns

shamatha   (calm) one of the two principal kinds of meditation in Buddhism; a method for obtaining the concentration and mental absorption known as DHYANA

shila   morality; keeping the basic precepts of Buddhist moral conduct

Siddhartha Gautama   The princely name of the last BUDDHA, son of the Shakya clan, who is said to have renounced his royalty in order to attain enlightenment

sutra (Sanskrit), sutta (Pali)   a Buddhist sacred text (whether oral or written) that is considered to be the words taught by the BUDDHA

Theravada The Teaching of the Elders, the dominant form of Buddhism practised today in such places as Sri Lanka, Burma and Thailand; said to be a more conservative form of Buddhism, and similar to that taught by the BUDDHA in India

vinaya the rules of monastic conduct practised by monks and nuns, thereby constituting the rules of the SANGHA

vipashyana (insight) one of the two principal kinds of meditation in Buddhism; aimed at the realization of PRAJNA, that is at enlightenment

CONFUCIANISM

Chun Qiu (Chun-ch'iu) *Springs and Autumns*, one of the Five Classics

Dong Zhongshu (Tung Chung-shu) 2nd-century BCE (HAN Dynasty) Confucian statesman and and philosopher

Han (Han) the name of the powerful dynasty (202BCE–220CE) under which Confucianism became elevated to the state cult

jing (ching) classic (written with a different Chinese character from the Daoist *jing*)

junzi (chün-tzu) prince, ruler; a word used by Confucius to mean a gentleman, a person exhibiting superior moral standards

Kong Fu Zi (K'ung Fu-tzu) Master Kong; Confucius

li (li) 1. ritual, ceremony; 2. reason, principle, as in the pre-existing principles behind the world and all the objects in it; 3. profit, advantage (in written Chinese there is no confusion between these three sets of meaning as they are written with different Chinese characters); compare QI

Li Ji (Li Chi) *Book of Rites*, one of the Five Classics

Mencius (Meng-tzu) a major RU philosopher of the 4th century BCE

Neo-Confucianism Confucian revival under the SONG Dynasty, incorporating elements of both Daoism and Buddhism

qi (ch'i) the principle that explains the physical universe; the material of which all things are made; see also under Daoism glossary

Qi (Ch'i) the name of a state

Qin (Ch'in) the name of a state; the dynasty (221–206BCE), preceding the HAN, which unified China and suppressed Confucianism

ren (jen) goodness, magnanimity, the supreme virtue of a gentleman (JUNZI)

Ru (ju) the school of philosophy founded by Confucius; Confucian, scholar

Shi Jing (Shih Ching) *Book of Songs* (or *Odes*), one of the Five Classics

shu (shu) reciprocity; closely connected with the idea of REN

Shu Jing (Shu Ching) *Book of History* (or *Documents*), one of the Five Classics

Song (Sung) the name of a state; the dynasty (960–1279CE) under which Confucianism regained its popular status; see also NEO-CONFUCIANISM

Tai Ji (T'ai-chi) the all-embracing LI of the universe, the Supreme Ultimate of the Neo-Confucians

Tian (T'ien) Heaven; emperors were believed to be mandated to rule by Heaven

xiao (hsiao) filial piety; the cornerstone of family, and thus social, order

Xun Zi (Hsün-tzu) a major RU philosopher of the 3rd century BCE

yang (yang) the principle (QI) of light, masculinity and movement; the opposite to YIN

yi (i or yi) righteousness, honour, loyalty; the outward manifestation of the qualities of the gentleman (JUNZI); often contrasted with LI (profit, advantage)

Yi Jing (I Ching or Yi Ching) *Book of Changes*, one of the Five Classics

yin (yin) the principle (QI) of darkness, femininity and quiescence; the opposite to YANG

Zhongguo (Chung-kuo) "central states", that is, China

Zhou (Chou) name of a state and of the dynasty (c.1027–256BCE) during which Confucius lived

Zhu Xi (Chu Hsi) 12th-century CE philosopher who expounded the revivalist movement known as NEO-CONFUCIANISM

zi (tzu) master

A NOTE ON THE PRONUNCIATION OF CHINESE

The Chinese names and terms in this book have been transcribed into the now standard form of romanization known as Pinyin. This differs from the older Wade-Giles system of transcription, with which some readers will be more familiar. The value of the following consonants should be noted:

Pinyin	Wade-Giles	Nearest English equivalent
c	tz'	ts in tsar
z	tz	dz in adze
j	ch	g in gin
zh	ch	j in job
q	ch'	ch in chin
x	hs	between s and sh
r	j	r (untrilled)

DAOISM

Cao Guojun (Ts'ao Kuo-chün) one of the Eight Immortals

dao (tao) path, way; the Way; the universal principle responsible for the creation of all things; the "non-being" (WU), which is at the basis of all "being"

Dao De Jing (Tao-te-ching) the best known and most revered of the Daoist classics, believed to have been written by LAO ZI

de (te) virtue, power; a quality, emanating from the DAO, which is at the core of every being

guan (kuan) larger type of Daoist temple, owned by priests or sects; compare ZISUN MIAO

Han (Han) see under Confucianism glossary

Han Xiang (Han Hsiang) one of the Eight Immortals

He Xiangu (Ho Hsien-ku) one of the Eight Immortals

Huang Di (Huang Ti) the Yellow Emperor

Ji Kang (Chi K'ang) one of the Seven Sages of the Bamboo Grove

jing (ching) vital essence; one of the three life-forces shared by humans and the cosmos; see also under Confucianism glossary

Kou Qianzhi (K'ou Ch'ien-chih) 5th-century Daoist Heavenly Master

Lan Caihe (Lan Ts'ai-ho) one of the Eight Immortals

Lao Zi (Lao-tzu) "old master"; Lao Zi, considered to be the founder of Daoism in the 6th or 5th century BCE

Li Xuan (Li Hsüan) "Iron Crutch", one of the Eight Immortals

Lie Zi (Lieh-tzu) 4th-century CE Daoist philosopher, writer of a Daoist classic

Lü Dongbin (Lü Tung-pin) one of the Eight Immortals

miao (miao) temple

Nü Gua (Nü Kua) creator goddess who presides on Kunlun Mountain

qi (ch'i) vapour, breath; one of the three life-forces shared by humans and the cosmos; the material from which all things are made; see also under Confucianism glossary

Ruan Ji (Juan Chi) one of the Seven Sages of the Bamboo Grove

Ruan Xian (Juan Hsien) one of the Seven Sages of the Bamboo Grove, nephew of RUAN JI

shen (shen) spirit; one of the three life-forces shared by humans and the cosmos; god

Shi Fang Conglin (Shih-fang-ts'ung-lin) "Ten Directions Grove", a type of Daoist community

Sima Qian (Ssu-ma Ch'ien) 2nd-century BCE (Han Dynasty) historian, author of *Historical Records*

Song (Sung) see under Confucianism glossary

Taiping Dao (T'ai-p'ing Tao) the Way of Great Peace; a major Daoist rebellion that broke out against government authorities and rapacious warlords toward the end of the HAN Dynasty

wu (wu) nothing; the non-being that is at the basis of being

wu wei (wu wei) Daoist principle of non-action; not indulging in useless effort; not doing anything that contradicts nature

Xi Wang Mu (Hsi-wang-mu) Queen Mother of the West, who presides over an abode of the immortals

xian (hsien) an immortal

yang (yang) see under Confucianism glossary

yin (yin) see under Confucianism glossary

Zhang Daoling (Chang Tao-ling) the leader of the 3rd-century CE Five Bushels of Rice Society, a Daoist regime that arose around the time of the collapse of the HAN Dynasty

Zhang Guo (Chang Kuo) one of the Eight Immortals

Zhang Jue (Chang Chüeh) the leader of the TAIPING DAO

Zhongli Quan (Chung-li Ch'uan) one of the Eight Immortals

Zhuang Zhou (Chuang Chou) the personal name of ZHUANG ZI

Zhuang Zi (Chuang-tzu) 3rd-century BCE Daoist philosopher, writer of one of the Daoist classics

zisun miao (tzu-sun miao) inherited temple; smaller, privately owned temple run by a Daoist master; compare GUAN

SHINTO

Amaterasu-omikami the sun goddess; the divine ancestor of the Japanese imperial family

gohei two strips of paper, each torn into four parts, that symbolize the presence of divinity; can also be made of metal

guji head priest of a Shinto shrine

Hachiman Shinto war god; reflects the KAMI of the semi-legendary Emperor Ojin

Ise-jingu site of the Grand Shrines of AMATERASU-OMIKAMI (Inner Shrine) and of the rice goddess (Outer Shrine)

Izumo-taisha site of the Grand Shrine of OKUNINUSHI

jingu see JINJA

jinja Shinto shrine

kami Shinto deity, god or spirit

kannushi Shinto priest

matsuri annual or biannual Shinto shrine festival

miko teenage shrine virgin, or "altar girl"; in ancient times *miko* were shamans

mikoshi portable or palanquin shrine carried around a neighbourhood or village on the shoulders of young men and women

oharai ritual purification

Okuninushi (Daikoku-sama) Great Lord of the Country, a major Shinto KAMI enshrined at IZUMO-TAISHA

oni Shinto demon

sakaki sacred pine branch with which purification rites are performed by a KANNUSHI

taisai major Shinto shrine festival, in which an image of the KAMI is placed in the MIKOSHI; held every second or third year in most neighbourhoods

Tengu long-nosed, benevolent "demon" who guards the MIKOSHI during a MATSURI

Tenrikyo a Shinto-based religion, founded in 1837 by a woman named Miki Nakayama

torii ceremonial gate marking the entrance to the sacred space of a shrine

FURTHER READING

HINDUISM

Bhagavad Gita Trans. Barbara Stoler Miller. New York: Columbia University Press, 1986.

Biardeau, Madeleine *Hinduism: The Anthropology of a Civilization*. Oxford: Oxford University Press, 1989.

Brockington, J. L. *The Sacred Thread: Hinduism in its Continuity and Diversity*. Edinburgh: Edinburgh University Press, 1981.

Doniger, Wendy, trans. *Hindu Myths: A Sourcebook Translated from the Sanskrit*. Harmondsworth: Penguin Books, 1975.

——. trans. *The Rig Veda: An Anthology*. New York: Penguin Books, 1981.

——. *Textual Sources for the Study of Hinduism*. Manchester: Manchester University Press, 1988.

Eck, Diana L. *Darsan: Seeing the Divine in India*. Chambersburg, PA: Anima Publications, 1985.

Embree, Ainslie T., ed. *Sources of Indian Tradition,* Vol. 1, *From the Beginning to 1800*. New York: Columbia University Press, 1988

Hume, R.E., trans. *The Thirteen Principal Upanishads*. Oxford: Oxford University Press, 1962.

Klostermaier, Klaus K. *A Survey of Hinduism*. Albany: State University of New York Press, 1994.

Lipner, Julius *The Hindus*. Oxford: Oxford University Press, 1994.

Radhakrishnan, S., and C.A. Moore, eds. *A Source Book in Indian Philosophy*. Princeton: Princeton University Press, 1957.

Waterstone, Richard *India*. London: Macmillan Reference Books, 1995; New York: Little, Brown, 1995.

Zaehner, R.C. *Myths and Symbols in Indian Art and Civilization*. Princeton: Princeton University Press, 1972.

Zimmer, Heinrich R., ed. *Philosophies of India*. New York: Meridan, 1956

BUDDHISM

Bechert, H., and R. Gombrich, eds. *The World of Buddhism*. London: Thames and Hudson, 1984; New York: Facts on File, 1984.

Boisselier J. *The Wisdom of the Buddha*. London: Thames and Hudson, 1994.

Carrithers, M. *The Buddha*. Oxford: Oxford University Press, 1986.

Conze, E. *A Short History of Buddhism*. London: Allen and Unwin Publishers, 1980.

——. *Buddhist Scriptures*. Harmondsworth: Penguin Books, 1959.

Gethin, R. *Buddhism*. Oxford: Oxford University Press, 1996.

Gombrich, R. *Theravada Buddhism*. London: Routledge, 1988

Harvey, P. *An Introduction to Buddhism*. Cambridge: Cambridge University Press, 1990.

Lowenstein, Tom *The Vision of the Buddha*. London: Macmillan Reference Books, 1995; New York: Little, Brown, 1995.

Powell A., and G. Harrison (photographs) *Living Buddhism*. London: British Museum Press, 1989.

Rahula, W. *What the Buddha Taught*. London: Gordon Frazer Gallery, 1967.

Saddhatissa, H. *The Buddha's Way*. London: Allen and Unwin Publishers, 1971.

Snellgrove, David *The Image of the Buddha*. Paris: Serindia, 1978.

——. *Indo-Tibetan Buddhism*. London: Serindia, 1985, and Berkeley: Shamabala, 1987.

Williams, P. *Mahayana Buddhism: its Doctrinal Foundations*. London: Routledge, 1989.

Zwalf, Wladimir *Buddhism: Art and Faith*. London: British Museum Press, 1985.

CONFUCIANISM

Chu Hsi *Learning to be a Sage*. Berkeley: University of California Press, 1990.

The Analects Trans. D.C. Lau. Harmondsworth: Penguin Books, 1979.

De Bary, William Theodore, ed. *Sources of the Chinese Tradition*. New York: Columbia University Press, 1960.

Fung Yu-lan *A Short History of Chinese Philosophy*. New York: The Macmillan Company, 1948.

The Book of Mencius Trans. D.C. Lau. Harmondsworth: Penguin Books, 1970.

Pound, Ezra *The Classical Anthology Defined by Confucius* (*The Shi Jing* or *Book of Songs*). Cambridge, Massachusetts: Harvard University Press, 1954.

Waley, Arthur *The Analects of Confucius*. London: George Allen and Unwin, 1938.

——. *The Book of Songs*. Boston and New York: Houghton Miflin, 1937.

——. *Three Ways of Thought in Ancient China*. London: George Allen and Unwin, 1939.

Watson, Burton *Early Chinese Literature*. New York: Columbia University Press, 1962.

——. trans. *Hsun-tzu: Basic Writings*. New York: Columbia University Press, 1962.

Yang, C.K. *Religion in Chinese Society*. Berkeley and Los Angeles: University of California Press, 1961.

DAOISM

Feuchtwang, Stephan *The Imperial Metaphor: Popular Religion in China*. London and New York: Routledge, 1992.

Fung Yu-lan *Chuang-tzu*. Beijing: Foreign Languages Press, 1989.

Goodrich, A.S. *The Peking Temple of the Eastern Peak*. Nagoya: Monumenta Serica, 1964.

Graham, A.C. *The Book of Lieh-tzu*. London: John Murray, 1960.

Lau, D.C. *Lao-tzu: Tao Te Ching*. Harmondsworth: Penguin Books, 1964.

Saso, Michael and David W. Chappell, eds. *Buddhist and Taoist Studies* 1. Honolulu: University of Hawaii Press, 1977.

Schipper, K.M. *The Taoist Body*. Berkeley: University of California Press, 1993.

Sivin, Nathan *Chinese Alchemism: Preliminary Studies*. Cambridge, Massachusetts: Harvard University Press, 1968.

Waley, Arthur *The Way and its Power*. London: George Allen and Unwin, 1939.

Watson, Burton *Chuang-tzu: Basic Writings*. New York: Columbia University Press, 1964.

Welch, Holmes and Anna Seidel, eds. *Facets of Taoism Essays on Chinese Religion*. New York and London: Yale University Press, 1979.

Yang, C.K. *Religion in Chinese Society*. Berkeley and Los Angeles: University of California Press, 1961.

SHINTO

Ashkenazi, Michael *Matsuri Festivals of a Japanese Town*. Honolulu: University of Hawaii Press, 1993.

Bellah, Robert *Tokugawa Religion: The Cultural Roots of Modern Japan*. New York: The Free Press, 1985.

Blacker, Carmen *The Catalpa Bow: A Study of Shamanistic Practices in Japan*. London: George Allen and Unwin, 1975.

Earhart, H. Byron *Japanese Religion: Unity and Diversity*. Belmont, CA: Wadsworth, 1982.

Hori, Ichiro *Folk Religion in Japan: Continuity and Change*. Chicago: University of Chicago Press, 1968.

Kageyama, Haruki *The Arts of Shinto*. Trans. Christine Guth. New York and Tokyo: Weatherhill, 1973.

Kato, Genichi *A Historical Study of the Religious Development of Shinto*. Trans. Shoyu Hanayama. New York: Greenwood Press, 1973.

——. *A Study of Shinto, the Religion of the Japanese Nation*. Tokyo: Meiji Japan Society, 1926

Kojiki Trans. Philippi, Donald L. Tokyo: University of Tokyo Press, 1968.

Lessa, William, A., and Evon Z. Vogt, eds. *A Reader in Comparative Religion: An Anthropological Approach*, (pp. 73–87). New York: Harper and Row, 1965.

Littleton, C. Scott "The Organization and Management of a Tokyo Shinto Shrine Festival" *Ethnology 25*, (pp.195–202): 1986.

Mason, J. W. T. *The Meaning of Shinto: The Primaeval Foundation of Creative Spirit in Modern Japan*. Washington, New York: Port Kennikat Press, 1965.

Nihongi: Chronicles of Japan from the Earliest Times to AD697. Trans. W. G. Aston. Rutland, VT: Tuttle, 1972.

Ono, Sokyo *Shinto: The Kami Way*. Rutland, VT: Tuttle, 1962.

Reader, Ian *Religion in Contemporary Japan*. Honolulu: University of Hawaii Press, 1991.

Spae, Joseph J. *Shinto Man*. Tokyo: Oriens Institute for Religious Research, 1972.

INDEX

PICTURE CREDITS

The publishers wish to thank the photographers and organizations for their kind permission to reproduce the following photographs in this book:

Abbreviations

A above; **B** below; **C** centre; **L** left; **R** right

AA&A Ancient Art and Architecture; **BAL** Bridgeman Art Library; **BM** British Museum; **BL** British Library; **DBP** Duncan Baird Publishers; **RHPL** Robert Harding Picture Library; **PP** Panos Pictures; **V&A** Victoria and Albert Museum

Endpapers BL; **1** Graham Harrison; **2** Ralph Clevenger/RHPL; **3** e.t. Archive; **7** e.t. Archive/BM; **8** M. Holford/Horniman Museum; **9** Christie's Colour Library, London; **11** M. Holford/Wellcome Institute; **13** DBP; **14–15** AA&A; **18–19** BL (Add 347); **19** Helene Rogers/TRIP; **20** BL (Or 4481 SR); **21** Gail Goodger/The Hutchison Library; **22** Images; **23** BL (Or 13758 12); **24** Wellcome Institute; **25** Ann & Bury Peerless; **26** The Hutchison Library; **27** Mary McGee; **28** Mecky Fogeling; **29** Images; **30** Krishna Centre of Consciousness, London; **31** BM (Or 19407 329); **32** Christophe Boisvieux; **33L** Helene Rogers/TRIP; **33R** Raghu Rai/Magnum; **34** AA&A; **35** BAL/V&A; **36** Images; **37** BAL/V&A; **38** Images; **39** Images; **40** M. Holford/Musée Guimet; **41** Roderick Johnson/Images of India; **42A** Ann & Bury Peerless; **42B** Mary McGee; **43** Jean-Leo Dugast/PP; **44** Mary McGee; **45** Images; **46** Dick Waghorne; **47** M. Harris/Tony Stone Images; **48–9** Grilly Bernard/Tony Stone Images; **50** Christophe Boisvieux; **51** Images of India; **52A** Mary McGee; **52B** Richard Lannoy; **53** Topham Picture Source; **54–5** China Photo Library; **58** RHPL; **59** University of Bristol; **60** BM/Barrett 37; **61** BM; **62** Ann & Bury Peerless; **63** Jean-Leo Dugast/PP; **64** Graham Harrison; **65** Ann & Bury Peerless; **66** Graham Harrison; **67** Jean-Leo Dugast/PP; **68** B. Barbey/Magnum; **69** Marc Riboud/Magnum; **70–71** China Photo Library; **72–3** Peter Adams; **75** Images; **76** BM (Or 5340); **77** Graham Harrison; **78** Peter Adams; **79** Mecky Fogeling; **80** Jean-Leo Dugast/PP; **81** Mecky Fogeling; **82** BM (Or 6902); **83** BL (Or 13926); **84** RHPL; **85** BM; **86** Graham Harrison; **87** BM; **88–9A** Lee Peters; **88–9B** Tradhart/David Hockney; **90** DBP; **90–91** G. Hellier/RHPL; **91** Catherine Platt/PP; **92–3** BL (15268); **96** C. M. Dixon; **97** BAL/V&A; **98** Images; **99** DBP; **100** Images; **101** RHPL; **103** BAL/BM; **106** RHPL; **107** RHPL; **108** John Chinnery; **110** e.t. Archive/Bibliothèque Nationale; **111** China Photo Library; **112A** John Chinnery; **112B** China Pictorial Press; **113** H. P. Merton/RHPL; **114** RHPL; **115** China Pictorial Press; **116–17** Alan Becker/Magnum; **120** Images; **121A** a/w Yukki Yaura; **121B** Images; **122** China Pictorial Press; **125** The Metropolitan Museum of Art, New York; **126** BAL; **127** *Alchemy and Chemistry*/DBP; **128** M. Holford/V&A; **129** *Alchemy and Chemistry*/DBP; **130–1** e.t. Archive; **132–3** TRIP; **134** RHPL; **135** Museum of Fine Art, Boston; **136** China Photo Library; **137L** Jacky Yip/China Photo Library; **137R** Images; **138A** Royal Asiatic Society, London; **138B** Christie's Colour Library; **139** Jean-Loup Charmet; **140A** RHPL; **140–41B** Christie's Colour Library; **142A** M. Holford/BM; **142B** Christie's Colour Library; **143** China Pictorial Press; **144–5** RHPL; **146** Hutchison Library; **148A** Nick Hadfield/Hutchison Library; **148B** DBP/Japanese Gallery, London; **149** RHPL; **150BL** C. Scott Littleton; **150R** e.t. Archive/Horniman Museum; **151** J Holmes/PP; **152–3** Images; **154A** J. Holmes/PP; **154B** RHPL; **155** Royal Asiatic Society; **156** Ernst Haas/Magnum; **157** M MacIntyre/Hutchison Library; **158A** Hutchison Library; **158B** Hutchison Library; **159** C. Scott Littleton; **161** BL (10270a); **176** Tony Stone Images

Every effort has been made to trace copyright holders. However, if there are any omissions we would be happy to rectify them in future editions.